THE
DEATH
OF
WESTERN
CHRISTIANITY

PATRICK SOOKHDEO

THE
DEATH
OF
WESTERN
CHRISTIANITY

DRINKING FROM THE POISONED WELLS
OF THE CULTURAL REVOLUTION

FOREWORD BY LORD CAREY
FORMER ARCHBISHOP OF CANTERBURY

The Death of Western Christianity: Drinking from the Poisoned Wells of the Cultural Revolution

First edition, October 2017

Published in the United States of America by Isaac Publishing

6729 Curran Street, McLean, Virginia 22101

Library of Congress Control Number: 2017953962

ISBN: 978-0-9977033-4-4

Printed in the United Kingdom

Contents

Look therefore carefully how ye walk,
not as unwise, but as wise;
redeeming the time,
because the days are evil.

Ephesians 5:15-16

(American Standard Version)

FOREWORD

This is a disturbing book. Many will not want to read it because they honestly know that it speaks truth to all Christians as we face the future. However, it is a book we MUST read if we want our churches to be visible, viable and vibrant places of hope and renewal.

Dr Sookhdeo acknowledges that for nearly 2,000 years the Church blazed strongly in the West, and, from a strong base in Europe, the rest of the world was evangelised. But, he contends: 'The fire is now dying. The flame is faintly flickering. It has burned down to the embers, though not extinguished.' This awoke a memory in me. When I became vicar of St Nicholas' Durham in 1975, I came across the diary of the church for 1925 and found that the Sunday school had numbered over 1,000 and when the Sunday school had its summer outing to places like Seaburn or Barnard Castle, the church hired a whole train. Fifty years later, however, in 1975 the Sunday school numbered less than 20. I could barely take in the scale of that decline.

In Europe, Christianity has played a profound role in shaping the values and aspirations, institutions and forms of our society throughout the ages. I believe that it has been an overwhelmingly positive influence and remains crucial today for the sense of moral purpose and shared endeavour of the Western nations.

But Dr Sookhdeo notes that the church is threatened by the forces of secularism, militant atheism, moral relativism, postmodernism, pluralism, hedonism, and individualism. Historic, creedal Christianity has been replaced by therapeutic consumerism. Sookhdeo contrasts this with the world's fastest growing religion – Islam, with its fixed sense of identity, its powerful symbols and 'pillars' and its strong sense of shared community encapsulated by the Arabic word *umma*. He calls upon the Western church to learn from persecuted Christians of the non-Western church and recover their creeds, commandments and community.

Though I do not wholly share his deep pessimism, I nevertheless believe that by and large his diagnosis of the causes of the decline of the Western church is correct. Indeed, this is a prophetic book which is a timely and telling indictment of all of us Western Christians. And Dr Sookhdeo's call to repentance, I hope will lead to a profound reassessment by Western church leaders. Only a commitment to our core beliefs, and a passionate engagement with and challenge to our culture will result in the revival and renewal of the church which we all long for.

GEORGE CAREY
Lord Carey of Clifton
103rd Archbishop of Canterbury

1
INTRODUCTION

The Church in the West once blazed strongly. For centuries, the Bible was at the heart of European culture and the cultures of North America and Australasia. Society at all levels recognised God at work in the world and gave allegiance, even if nominally, to the Lord Jesus Christ. From the stronghold of 'Christendom,' the Gospel was carried across the globe.

The fire is now dying. The flame is faintly flickering. It has burned down to the embers, though not extinguished.

In pockets, the Church burns brightly. Many evangelical and Pentecostal churches are growing. Christianity burns strongly in the Caribbean and amongst Afro-Caribbean communities in the diaspora. Eastern Europe Catholics remain robust in their faith a generation after communism ended, and bring the blaze with them when they move to western Europe, North America or Australasia. Middle Eastern Orthodox Christian refugees show their Western hosts that they are not ashamed of their faith.

Sadly, these are exceptions. *The Christian Post* reported a 2017 study revealing that for each person in the UK brought up with no religion who later embraces Christianity, there are 26 people brought up as Christians who turn agnostic or atheist. In 2011, *The Independent* estimated that as many as 5,000 British people convert to Islam every year. The Western Church is rapidly declining and, if trends continue, many who are reading these pages in 2017 — the 500th anniversary of the Reformation — will live to see it die — unless God graciously intervenes.

Why is Christianity dying? When a fish goes bad, the rot starts at the head and then spreads to the body. Since the 1960s, Christian leaders have progressively betrayed the Gospel. The starkest example of this is aping the culture to affirm, bless and engage in pansexual lifestyles. This, lamentably, is merely one example of a wide-ranging liberalism that readily bends the beliefs of historic Christianity to avoid any confrontation with secular society. Many ordinary Christians, clergy and pastors struggle to remain faithful, but they are betrayed by the treachery of the hierarchy.

In 1517, Martin Luther nailed his 95 Theses to the church door in Wittenberg, sparking off the Reformation. Luther was doubly troubled by corruption within the Church and the Ottoman armies marching across Europe under the banner of Islam.

Half a millennium later, the same twin threats confront the Church in the West, albeit this time Islam is advancing by mostly non-violent means. There is also a third threat that Luther did not have to face — humanism.

The New Civic Religion (Patrick Sookhdeo, 2016) charts the trajectory of the bold yet subtle strategy of humanism. The humanist leaders were zealous and creative evangelists, surpassing the fervour of Christian missionaries. The results are now plainly visible. In less than a generation, the humanists successfully uprooted Western culture from its Judaeo-Christian foundation on rock and transplanted it to a humanist edifice built on sand.

Humanism atomised Western society to the cult of fragmented individualism, making the word society sound strange and unfamiliar. Humanism bulldozed Biblical morality and replaced it with licensed permissiveness. Humanism offered a new distorted prism through which the brave new West could view the Church. Christians were no longer seen as the 'good guys' but as the 'bad guys' or at best the 'laughably foolish guys.'

The Old Testament prophets condemned 'those who call evil good and good evil' (Isaiah 5:20). A more accurate description of our society is not possible. The leadership of Anglo-Saxon Christianity charge down the hill like the Gadarene swine, eager to keep up with or even outdo contemporary culture as it swiftly dissolves into decadence. We are seeing the horrifying prophetic vision of debauchery in the Jerusalem Temple where the 70 elders continued their placid worship while the walls were crawling with forbidden and detestable animals (Ezekiel 8:6-11).

Western Christianity has sold its identity for a mess of pottage. Christians no longer know who they are and so cannot withstand the multipronged attacks on their faith. People who have forgotten their past have no hope of a future. We will examine this all-important loss of Christian identity in Chapter 8.

Meanwhile, we grasp at metaphors to describe the comatose and life-threatening nature of the Church's predicament. The Church has been poisoned. The flames have been doused and all but quenched. The rot is endemic.

> Christianity is decaying and going down the gutter because the God of modern Christianity is not the God of the Bible.
> — A. W .Tozer (1897-1963)

On 8 April 1966, *Time* magazine's cover page shouted out a three-word question: 'Is God Dead?' The death of God article asked if religion in general and Christianity in particular was relevant in an age where communism, science and technology were making great strides. Then,

97% of Americans believed with absolute certainly in the existence of God. Fifty years later, that number has been whittled down to 63%, says a Pew study. God may not be dead, but Christianity is dying out across the Western world (Lipka, 2015).

The projections are alarming. Popular publications scream out scary headlines. 'Christians are leaving the faith in droves and the trend isn't slowing down' (*Business Insider*, 28 April 2015); 'US Christians numbers "decline sharply"' (*BBC News*, 12 May 2015); 'Church attendance drops to lowest rate EVER as UK faces "anti-Christian" culture' (*The Express*, 13 January 2016) and '2067: The end of British Christianity' (*The Spectator*, 13 June 2015).

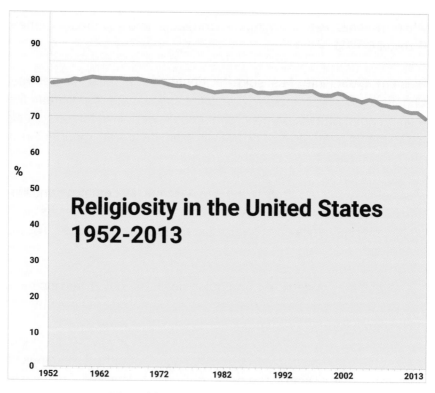

Adapted from Aggregate Religiosity Index,
updated from Grant, *Sociological Spectrum*, 2008

One of the most comprehensive studies measuring the religiosity of the United States from 1952 to 2013, was conducted by sociologist Professor Tobin Grant (Grant, 2014). After reviewing a number of measures of religiosity based on information about attendance at worship services, church membership figures, prayer, and feelings toward religion, Grant concluded that the United States is in the midst of what he described as the 'the Great Decline.' Grant contrasts this with the period he calls the 'the Great Awakening' shortly after the end of the Second World War, during which Christianity experienced a revival of sorts.

American Christianity nosedived in the 1960s and 1970s, partly as a reaction to the Vietnam War. People began to question authorities and institutions, Church and state. After the 1970s, Christianity in the US remained relatively stable until the turn of the millennium. Since then, Christianity has plummeted far more sharply than in the 1960s and 1970s, and twice as fast. The number of atheists and 'nones' (people who are not atheist but who have no religious affiliation) is growing dramatically. Christianity plays far less of a role than in any other period since the 1950s. Correspondingly, the number of those professing belief in Christianity is plunging at an alarming rate, not just in the US, but right across the West.

In the UK, fewer children are being born into families calling themselves Christian. The British census found that the number fell by 5.3 million between 2001 and 2011. 'One day the last native-born Christian will die and that will be that,' commented *The Spectator*, calculating that, if 2015 rates of decline continued, Anglicanism would disappear from Britain by 2033 and indigenous Christianity by 2067. According to the British Social Attitudes survey, in 1983 over two-thirds of the population said they were Christian, but in 2017 this figure was down to 41% while 53% said they had no religion. In 1983, 40% of the population identified themselves as Anglican; by 2017 this had fallen to 15% (3% for the 18-24 age range). Between 2012 and 2014 some 1.7 million souls abandoned the Church of England, averaging 16,000 per week. (Thompson, 2015; Rudgard, 2017)

In March 2016, the British Mennonites held their last service, ending 400 years of history. Ed Sherit, a Mennonite elder, explained, 'As with many Christian churches, we failed to convince the next generation that following Jesus is the best way. We lost the next generation.' Reporting on the Church shutting its doors forever *The Guardian* (Sherwood, 2016) commented, 'Another factor in the church's decline was the changing attitudes towards religion in society generally. In the 2011 census about a quarter of the UK population reported that they had no religion, up more than 10 percentage points since the previous census in 2001.'

A significant proportion of the declining UK Christian population describing themselves as belonging to the Church of England admit to being 'cultural' Christians. The actual attendance figures of the Church of England paint a dismal picture. In 2016, the number of people attending weekly services dropped to below one million for the first time (about two percent of the population). Even this figure is an overestimate as it includes the same people who attend multiple services during the week. Those attending Anglican services fell by 12% between 2004 and 2014. Speaking at the Anglican primates' meeting in Canterbury 2014, Archbishop of Canterbury Justin Welby admitted that he did not expect a change in the trend soon despite ambitious and strategic interventions:

> In some parts of the Communion decline in numbers has been a pattern for many years. In England our numbers have been falling at about 1% every year since [World War Two] ... The culture [is] becoming anti-Christian, whether it is on matters of sexual morality, or the care for people at the beginning or the end of life. It is easy to paint a very gloomy picture.

Reacting to the attendance figures, Keith Porteous Wood, Executive Director of the National Secular Society, said, in a comment reported by *The Guardian*:

> Church of England attendance now appears to have fallen below 2% of the population, and looks set to fall further given

the preponderance of older churchgoers. This seriously calls into question its right to remain the established church. Indeed, it is inappropriate for there to be any established religion in a modern pluralistic society, far less one where the majority do not consider themselves to be religious.

The decline in membership is not limited to the Church of England. In 2015, membership of all denominations combined was 10.3% of the population. However, church attendance in all denominations was barely five percent. The Church of England accounted for almost half of all Christians attending church in England.

On 17 January 2016, *The Times* announced, 'A post-Christian era has dawned in Britain.' Those claiming to have no religion rose from 37% of the population in 2013 to 42% in 2015 to 46% in 2016 with only 31% claiming to be Christian. The survey noted that the figures would be much worse for Christianity if not for the influx of Christian migrants from Africa and Eastern Europe.

In Australia, the 2016 census revealed that just over 52% of the country was Christian (down from 88% in 1966). In the previous five years, the Muslim and Hindu populations had each increased by more than 100,000 (now 2.6% and 1.9% respectively). Nearly 30% of respondents said they had no religion. (Berlinger, 2017)

In Norway, a 2016 Ipsos study revealed that those who did not believe in God outnumbered those who did for the first time ever in the nation's history. To the question 'Do you believe in God?' 39% responded 'No' while 37% said 'Yes.' The remainder did not know. Two years earlier, those answering 'yes' and 'no' to this question were equal in number and in 1985 only 20% of the population said they did not believe in God. This tidal wave of atheism and secularism is responsible for increased resistance to Christianity in Norway. In 2015, the Norwegian government asked all facilities for asylum seekers to remove crosses, images of Jesus and other Christian symbols, in case such items caused offence to non-Christians.

In Iceland, a traditionally Christian country, people are abandoning the Church *en masse*. According to a Gallup poll (*The Washington Post* 23 January 2016), 90% of the population claimed to be Christian in 1996. In just 20 years, this figure had fallen to 46%. In the same period, non-believers rose from 13% to 54%. The poll did not identify a single respondent who believed that God created the earth. Bjarni Jonsson, Managing Director of the Icelandic Ethical Humanist Association, commented on Christianity's catastrophic decline in Iceland: 'Secularization has occurred very quickly, especially among younger people. With increased education and broad-mindedness, change can occur quickly.'

In 2014, a Gallup survey on religiosity identified Sweden as the least religious country after China. China had decades of atheist communist rule; Sweden is a country with a strong Christian heritage. Only eight percent of Swedes attend a religious service and those go do so very occasionally, at Christmas and Easter. The Swedish government website has a page titled '10 Fundamentals of Religion in Sweden' explaining Sweden's secularisation:

> Sweden is a highly secular nation and Swedes appear to see little connection between religiosity and happiness. According to The Global Index of Religiosity and Atheism (2012), only 29 per cent of Swedes claim to be religious, compared with 59 per cent globally. These figures rank Sweden as one of the least religious countries in the world. Not all Swedes are comfortable with the at times prominent cultural role of the church either, and many people pursue alternative forms of ritual. With marriages on the rise in Sweden, civil weddings now account for nearly a third of all marriage ceremonies. In addition, secular 'name-giving' ceremonies (*namngivningsceremonier*) for infants also exist, with the aim of celebrating the arrival of a new child without the religious overtones of a christening.

The website goes on to explain how much secularisation has affected not only society but also the Church.

Christianity and the church may have maintained ritual and cultural importance in Sweden, but this has not prevented the country from becoming one of the world's most liberal societies. In some areas where religious and social conservatism often prevail, such as the right to abortion, no serious debate exists in Sweden. Living together and having children without being married is also socially acceptable, and recent statistics suggest that more than 40 per cent of first-time parents in Sweden have children before getting married. The Church of Sweden has often accompanied liberal social change rather than obstructing it. For example, in 2009 the church decided to begin performing same-sex marriage ceremonies as Sweden legalised same-sex marriage in the same year. At the end of 2014, 5,356 women and 4,212 men had married a person of the same sex. Traditional yet new thinking, secular yet religious, tolerant yet challenging — it all holds true for Sweden.

The *National Geographic* article 'The World's Newest Major Religion: No Religion,' describes the rise of the religiously unaffiliated, or 'nones,' who now constitute the second largest 'religious' group in North America and Western Europe. 'Nones' make up a quarter of the American population and have overtaken Catholics, mainline Protestants and followers of all non-Christian faiths combined.

There have long been predictions that religion would fade from relevancy as the world modernizes, but all the recent surveys are finding that it's happening startlingly fast. France will have a majority secular population soon. So will the Netherlands and New Zealand. The United Kingdom and Australia will soon lose Christian majorities. Religion is rapidly becoming less important than it's ever been, even to people who live in countries where faith has affected everything from rulers to borders to architecture. (Bullard, 2016)

The death throes of Christianity are significantly affecting the social fabric of the West. The article points out that this realignment towards atheism has profound outcomes on how people view the world, how they regard death, how they act towards others and how they raise their children. The Western church is losing, or in most countries has already lost, the battle over abortion, euthanasia, prayer in schools and same-sex marriage.

We have entered the 'post-Christian' era. The German philosopher Hermann von Keyserling first used the term in his book *America Set Free* (1929). The term regained popularity in the 1960s following the 'death of God' movement. A group of theologians, recognising the decline in a belief in God, argued that for Christianity to survive it would have to do so without an orthodox understanding of God.

Today, the Church is scarcely distinguishable from society. Rod Dreher, author of *The Benedict Option: A Strategy for Christians in a Post-Christian Nation* (2017), writes that we entered 'the new Dark Age.' There is hardly any difference between the behaviour of Christians and non-Christians in the West, as we will see in Chapter 3. Christians are as likely, and in some cases more likely, to have sex before or outside marriage, lie, cheat, steal, divorce and pursue materialism than their non-Christian counterparts.

As early as the 18th century, John Wesley, founder of Methodism, had warned of this compliance. 'What one generation tolerates the next generation will embrace.'

In the span of a single lifetime, Europe and the Western world have become almost unrecognisable. Society is hurtling towards hell in a handbasket of moral debauchery. Christians who hold conservative views are seen as dangerous to society.

A relativism that is not only post-Christian but inherently and intentionally anti-Christian has replaced Christianity. This relativism has demolished Christian virtues and labelled them unenlightened, backward, intolerant, sexist, exclusivist, bigoted, homophobic, transphobic, Islamophobic, and, in some cases, illegal. The tables have been upturned as social mores once regarded as immoral and sinful under the influence of Christianity, are now normalised and celebrated.

This has left the Church facing a fatal crisis of identity. Desperate to survive and remain relevant, it has struck a Faustian bargain with postmodern Western ideals, tolerating and taking on unorthodox beliefs and behaviours. This has, in fact, produced the opposite effect, alienating even more people and making the Church an object of ridicule. In fact, evidence from recent studies suggests that liberal churches die fastest.

> In the Western world in particular, where Christianity is marginalized and secular culture dismisses it as an ideological has-been, where daily we rub shoulders with persons of other faiths and of no faith, and where within the older Protestant churches tolerating the intolerable is advocated as a requirement of justice, versions of Christianity that care more for experiences of life than for principles of truth will neither strengthen churches nor glorify God.... The well-being of Christianity worldwide for this twenty-first century directly depends, I am convinced, on the recovery of what has historically been called catechesis – that is, the ministry of systematically teaching people in and coming into our churches the sinew-truths that Christians live by, and the faithful, practical, consistent way for Christians to live by them.
> — J. I. Packer (2008)

Worse still, the West exports its increasingly immoral values and ideals across the world. Such 'activism' is provoking violent extremist groups, especially from conservative religions like Islam, to challenge this assault on traditional morality. There is no excuse for such violence, but Westerners need to understand that these groups justify their violence as a holy war on a morally bankrupt West. In 2016, Baroness Sayeeda Warsi, a prominent lawyer and the first Muslim woman appointed to a UK cabinet position, expressed her deep belief in Britain's need to return to its Christian roots and a 'Europe that is sure about its Christian heritage.' 'For minority faiths to feel truly comfortable about who they are, the majority has got to be sure about who it is,' she added.

On the night of 13 November 2015, a series of seven coordinated attacks rocked the city of Paris. Over 130 people were killed, many more seriously injured. That night's deadliest attack was at a rock concert. Three gunmen with assault rifles entered the Boulevard Voltaire and began firing indiscriminately into the crowd, killing 89 and wounded over 100 revellers. The band from California performing that night was the *Eagles of Death Metal*. The terrorists opened fire as the band was leading the crowd in singing a song called 'Kiss the Devil.'

> Who'll love the devil?
> Who'll sing his song?
> Who will love the devil and his song?
> I'll love the devil, I'll sing his song
> I will love the devil and his song
> Who'll love the devil?
> Who'll kiss his tongue?
> Who will kiss the devil on his tongue?
> I'll love the devil I'll kiss his tongue
> I will kiss the devil on his tongue

Soon after the attack, the band released a statement on social media talking about their 'prayers for those affected in these tragic events.' A band that sings satanic lyrics later offers prayers for the victims of the attack without any apparent irony.

On 22 May 2017, a terrorist detonated his bomb at an Ariana Grande pop concert in Manchester, England. In 'Side to Side' Grande sang, 'Tonight I'm making deals with the devil/ And know it's going to get me in trouble... Let them hoes know.' Grande is famous for promoting 'raunch' culture. Masquerading as a liberation movement for girls in their early teens, her music appears to be grooming girls for 'consequence-free sex.' Many of Grande's songs and videos simulate pansexual promiscuity. Yet many parents permit and even encourage their teenage daughters to attend her concerts and endorse the raunch culture and lifestyle.

After the Manchester bombing, journalist Alexis Petridis explained in his column for *The Guardian* why he took his daughters aged seven and ten to such concerts. 'I take them because I think those big pop gigs do something incredibly important.' Recalling the first time he took his older daughter, then aged seven, to a concert, he wrote, '... it was the way it gave her a first glimpse of a world that was previously outside her experience, a more adult, or at least more mature world than the one she knew, a world that would one day be her own, and how excited she was to see it, how — as she put it — grown-up it made her feel.' For Petridis, 'Music aimed at teenage girls is derided but the likes of Ariana Grande provide the kind of empowering, transcendent experience that terrorists hate.'

Cultural analysist, Jenny Taylor, added her critique of the dangers of raunch culture in the aftermath of the Manchester attack.

> That the dark excess stalking such entertainment events contributed to a moral and social atmosphere in which wholesale sex grooming was able to take place without public comment for two whole decades seems to have escaped the sentimentalists' notice. Sexuality was something that used to be held to need the constraints of parents and guardians and society as a whole. Now parents ferry their children to these spectacles.

Two weeks after the Manchester attack, pop-star Justin Bieber made a speech during a charity performance in support of the Manchester victims. *God TV* reported the story under the headline 'Justin Bieber Preaches at Manchester Benefit Concert.' *Christian Today* ran a similar story, praising the celebrity Katy Perry (who sings 'I kissed a Girl and Liked It') for her tweet 'praying for everyone @ArianaGrande's show' and extolling Grande who led a prayer backstage before the benefit concert. Ruth Gledhill, editor of *Christian Today*, described the concert as 'imbued with a sense of godliness, and the power of good to triumph ultimately in the face of evil.'

If the evangelical media can uncritically endorse raunch culture celebrities like Grande and Perry and can applaud Justin Bieber, who lives the sex, drink, drugs and rock and roll lifestyle to its fullest, the Church in the West is well and truly trapped in the dungeons of its own decadence.

2
WESTERN CULTURE TODAY

In the moral realm, there is very little consensus left in Western countries over the proper basis of moral behaviour. And because of the power of the media, for millions of men and women the only venue where moral questions are discussed and weighed is the talk show, where more often than not the primary aim is to entertain, even shock, not to think. When Geraldo and Oprah become the arbiters of public morality, when the opinion of the latest media personality is sought on everything from abortion to transvestites, when banality is mistaken for profundity because [it is] uttered by a movie star or a basketball player, it is not surprising that there is less thought than hype. Oprah shapes more of the nation's grasp of right and wrong than most of the pulpits in the land. Personal and social ethics have been removed from the realms of truth and structures of thoughts; they have not only been relativized, but they have been democratized and trivialized. — D.A. Carson (2011)

Ours is a post-Christian world in which Christianity, not only in the number of Christians but in cultural emphasis and cultural result, is no longer the consensus or ethos of our society – Francis Schaeffer (1984)

Culture is the collective beliefs, values, worldview and way of life specific to a group of people. Distinctive cultural elements include norms, symbols, heroes, language, rituals, practices, dress and more. Dutch social psychologist Geert Hofstede defines culture as 'the collective programming of the mind that distinguishes the members of one group or category of people from others.'

What are the ideologies, philosophies and worldviews responsible for the 'collective programming' of the Western mind in a post-Christian age?

ATHEISM

Western culture has shifted from a Christian worldview to a culture that is not merely indifferent to God, but militantly campaigns against belief in a supernatural or transcendent being. The cultural Marxist philosopher György Lukács summed it up as a refusal 'to accept the world as something that has arisen (or e.g. has been created by God) independently of the knowing subject,' preferring 'to conceive of it instead as its own product.'

Over the last half a century, militant atheists have creatively camouflaged atheism as 'humanism' and vigorously promoted it in schools. An indoctrinated younger generation has bought widely into believing that God does not exist, this life is all that there is, humans are the pinnacle of an evolutionary process, and that 'religion poisons everything' – the sub-title of a bestselling book by British atheist Christopher Hitchens. A belief in the non-existence of God affects how people view the world, themselves, others, marriage, family, sexuality, the meaning of life and their purpose in the world. If there is no God, afterlife or consequence for one's actions, a sense of self-importance increases, as does the pursuit of sensual pleasures. As Russian novelist Fyodor

Dostoevsky wrote in *The Brothers Karamazov* (1880), 'If God does not exist, everything is permitted.'

Hitchens, along with Oxford biologist Richard Dawkins. American philosopher and neuroscientist Sam Harris, and American philosopher and cognitive scientist Daniel Dennett have come to be known as the 'four horsemen of the atheist apocalypse.'

What do atheists look like? In 2015, the Atheist Alliance International reported on the demographic makeup of atheists stating that the majority of atheists are Western, white (78%), middle class, university educated, men (68%). According to an earlier 2012 report from the Pew Research Center on Religion and Public Life, only 3% of US atheists and agnostics were black, 6% were Hispanic, and 4% were Asian. Some 82% were white. Not surprisingly, Dawkins, Hitchens, Harris and Dennett are all white, university educated, Western men.

New Testament scholar Craig Keener, after a comprehensive study of miracles in a wide variety of cultures, concludes that routinely rejecting the possibility of the supernatural is a deeply Eurocentric impulse.

Atheists are addressing this lack of diversity and trying to spread their ideology across racial, gender, social and educational boundaries. In the above 2015 report, they even suggest co-opting the 'ongoing implementation of the UN System Wide Action Plan on Gender Equality and the Empowerment of Women' as one strategy to promote atheism. (Diaz & Hamill, 2015) This exposes the United Nations' involvement in spreading atheism, albeit thinly veiled by the noble cause of gender equality.

MORAL RELATIVISM

The idea of God is the type and foundation of the principle of authority and absolutism, which it is our task to destroy or at least to subordinate wherever it manifests itself. — Pierre-Joseph Proudhon, humanist, economist and philosopher (1846)

'What you believe is true for you. What I believe is true for me.' The view expressed in such a statement is called relativism. What may be right for one person in one situation can be wrong for another person in the same situation or the same person in another situation. It is not for anyone to question or judge the behaviour, actions and decisions of anyone else.

For many Westerners, absolute right and wrong no longer exist. In the US, the roots of this worldview go as far back as 1932 as seen in the report of the *Character Education Committee of American Association of School Administrators*, which was to form the basis of a morally relativist culture in the coming decades.

> Relativity must replace absolutism in the realm of morals as well as in the spheres of physics and biology. This of course does not involve the denial of the principle of continuity in human affairs. Nor does it mean that each generation must repudiate the system of values of its predecessors. It does mean, however, that no such system is permanent; that it will have to change and grow in response to experience — Character Education Committee (1932)

The chickens of moral relativism have come home to roost with the 2016 Barna survey, *The End of Absolutes: America's New Moral Code*, revealing more than half the US population to be moral relativists. Fifty-seven percent of Americans believe that defining what is right or wrong is a matter of personal experience. Seventy-four percent of millennials (those born between 1980-2000) believe that morality is relative, agreeing with the statement, 'whatever is right for your life works best for you is the only truth you can know.' This figure is three times higher than that for those born before 1945. The study credits the school curriculum for this shift and concludes:

Christianity has for the most part been removed as the moral norm of culture and replaced with a new moral code, which consists of six tenets:

1. The best way of finding yourself is by looking within yourself.

2. People should not criticize someone else's life choices.

3. To be fulfilled in life, you should pursue the things you desire most.

4. The highest goal of life is to enjoy it as much as possible.

5. People can believe whatever they want, as long as those beliefs don't affect society.

6. Any kind of sexual expression between two consenting adults is acceptable. (Haverluck, 2016)

POSTMODERNISM

> [In] the multidimensional and slippery space of post-modernism anything goes with anything, like a game without rules. Floating images ... maintain no relationship with anything at all, and meaning becomes detachable like the keys on a key ring. Dissociated and decontextualized, they slide past one another failing to link up into a coherent sequence. Their fluctuating but not reciprocal interactions are unable to fix meaning. — Painter, author and professor Suzy Gablik speaking on how postmodernism is expressed in art. (Callincos, 1989)

Postmodernism is linked to moral relativism but goes deeper. Moral relativism rejects moral absolutes; postmodernism rejects all absolutes. Indeed, the very idea of absolute truth is considered fiction. Worse still, truth claims are in reality claims to power. Truth is subjective and plural. Consequently, there is no fixed meaning to text, authority, thought, norm or reality. Everything, including the Bible, is open to multiple interpretations. No interpretation can be final or definitive. Our view of reality is entirely a matter of perspective. Individuals construct their own truths. Reason is suspect. Feelings trump facts. Experience and emotion supersede empiricism or reality.

Postmodernism is Pontius Pilate personified, mockingly asking Jesus, 'What is truth?' (John 18:38).

A postmodern society permits everything and prohibits nothing. The only taboo is to declare something taboo.

PLURALISM

Pluralism is the view that all cultures, religions, beliefs, norms and practices are equally valid — even if they contradict each other. For a culture to claim it is better than another culture is cultural imperialism. Faced with the diversity of many races, religions, cultures and beliefs, pluralists insist that pluralism is the only path to peaceful coexistence. Most postmodernists are also pluralist.

Pluralism celebrates diversity and dialogue between cultures and religions. However, far from pursuing the noble virtue of tolerance as might be expected, pluralism enforces a reductionist and minimalist lowest common denominator between cultures and religions. Its iron fist of uniformity thus destroys the distinctiveness of all religions and cultures.

Pluralism is eroding the Judaeo-Christian basis of the Western legal system and compelling new legislation against Christians and in favour of minority cultures and religions. At the same time, pluralism ignores harmful cultural practices like Female Genital Mutilation (FGM), child brides, polygamy, forced marriage and harmful religious practices like punishment for apostasy. Immigrant communities in the West are increasingly importing and following these practices.

Muslim communities are pressurizing governments to make sharia (Islamic law) part of the legislation of Australia, Austria, Canada, Denmark, Finland, France, Germany, Ireland, the Netherlands, Sweden, the UK and the USA. In 2014, the UK had approximately 85 sharia courts operating in Muslim-majority areas.

The incompatibility and contradictions between most religions, ideologies and philosophical systems expose pluralism as fundamentally flawed and unworkable. The Bible declares Jesus Christ to be Lord and God, while the Quran insists that Jesus is merely a prophet. These two positions are incompatible and irreconcilable. Both cannot be true.

HEDONISM

Hedonism is the pursuit of pleasure for pleasure's sake. Pleasure is seen as life's ultimate goal. Hedonism is a logical outcome of atheism. If there is neither God, nor afterlife, this life should be lived to its fullest. Unbridled sensual pleasure becomes a substitute for the happiness, meaning and fulfilment that comes from a relationship with God. Anything that causes pain, discomfort or inconvenience must be eliminated. Pleasure is no longer a desire; it becomes a right.

Some of the ancient Greeks and Romans, famous for their orgies, and some Hindu sects, practised hedonism. In recent times, hedonism has expanded exponentially in the West. Advances in medicine and technology have dramatically improved the standard of living in Western countries. The welfare state has made it possible for people to enjoy benefits without responsibilities. Never before in history has there been so much disposable income and leisure time available to so many individuals. The credit card facilitates instant gratification. 'I want it and I want it now.' The downside has been the rise of staggering personal and national debt. Westerners are living lifestyles that many of them can ill afford.

The ultimate hedonistic goal is to abolish all suffering, as scientist David Pearce, writing in 2014, envisioned on a grand scale.

> The Hedonistic Imperative outlines how genetic engineering and nanotechnology will abolish suffering in all sentient life. This project is ambitious but technically feasible. It is also instrumentally rational and ethically mandatory. The metabolic pathways of pain and malaise evolved only because they once served the fitness of our genes. They will be replaced by a different sort of neural architecture. States of sublime well-being are destined to become the genetically pre-programmed norm of mental health. The world's last aversive experience will be a precisely dateable event.

CONSUMERISM AND MATERIALISM

> We must shift America from a needs, to a desires culture ... People must be trained to desire, to want new things even before the old had been entirely consumed. We must shape a new mentality in America. Man's desires must overshadow his needs — Paul Mazur of Lehman Brothers (1927)

Materialism is the belief that nothing exists except matter. Hence, matter is all that matters and possessions bring happiness. Materialism has become a key feature of Western culture. A person's worth is measured by what they can acquire. The materialist pursues possessions such as fast cars, luxury yachts, large houses, technological gadgets, exotic holidays, gourmet food and designer clothes as the main aim of life, rather than goals such as character development, service to humanity, generosity, righteousness, wisdom and close relationships with others.

Materialism leads to increased stress, depression, higher risks of smoking, high blood pressure and cholesterol, inactivity, obesity, heart disease, diabetes and cancer. (Bunker, Colquhoun, Esler, et al, 2003)

The consequence of materialism is consumption. In 1927, Paul Mazur a Wall Street banker wrote:

> A change has come over our democracy, it is called consumptionism. The American citizen's first importance to his country is now no longer that of citizen, but that of consumer. (Mazur, 1927)

I buy, therefore I am. Shop until you drop. Advertising and marketing are the handmaidens of consumerism. They target consumers by creating a dissatisfaction not only with what we have, but with who we are. They constantly peddle a message of restlessness, and an unquenchable desire for happiness and pleasure.

We are told we deserve more 'because I'm worth it,' as in the advertisement for cosmetic products from L'Oréal. This creates a sense of entitlement.

Materialism and consumerism are obsessively self-centred and this links them to individualism.

INDIVIDUALISM

> Individualism regards man — every man — as an independent, sovereign entity who possesses an inalienable right to his own life, a right derived from his nature as a rational being. Individualism holds that a civilized society, or any form of association, cooperation or peaceful coexistence among men, can be achieved only on the basis of the recognition of individual rights — and that a group, as such, has no rights other than the individual rights of its members — Ayn Rand, *The Virtue of Selfishness* (2017)

Individualism is a dominant and unique feature of Western society. Individualism promotes the freedoms, rights and choices of the individual over those of the family or community.

Political philosopher Larry Siedentop, in his carefully argued book *Inventing the Individual: The Origins of Western Liberalism*, explains how the 'individual' became the organizing principle of society in the West. He argues that the fundamental moral equality of individuals was pioneered by Christian thinkers of the Middle Ages who drew on the moral revolution carried out by the early church. The individual gradually displaced the claims of family, tribe, and caste as the basis of social organization. This led to a liberating belief in individual freedom, in the fundamental moral equality of individuals, in a legal system based on equality, and in a representative form of government befitting a society of free people — laying the foundation for liberal democracy in the West.

Most cultures in Asia, Africa and the Middle East are communitarian. They privilege the needs of the group above the needs of the individual. Individual rights are overlooked in a communitarian society. Couples are forced into arranged marriages. Voters cast their ballot for a candidate simply because the politician belongs to their caste or tribe.

However, as Christianity dies the individual loses his or her anchor and is cut adrift on a vast ocean of aloneness. 'Thinking *for* ourselves' is redefined as 'thinking *of* ourselves.' Autonomy (the ability to act according to our internalized values and beliefs) is confused with independence (not being reliant on or influenced by others). (Echersley, 2005)

Without God, individuals are forced to re-invent their identity. This is why so many in Western society are confused about who they are and why so much energy and effort is spent in searching for the meaning of life and their place in the world.

Without community or family ties, people in individualistic societies feel alone and uncertain. Everyone else is a competitor, and so success and even survival in the world are a result of individual efforts. This creates high levels of stress and issues of self-worth. The drive to be even more independent and selfish becomes a matter of self-preservation and survival, resulting in a dog-eat-dog world.

With the focus on self comes the worship of self. There is no clearer illustration of this than the 'selfie' generation who constantly photograph themselves and post the 'selfies' online. Jessica Schirripa, writing in 2015 on 'How This Generation's Obsession With Selfies Correlates With Mental Disorders,' quotes clinical and political psychologist Bart Rossi:

> Today too many people are interested in making a statement about themselves on the internet and creating an influential existence. Selfies, when used to excess, show a lack of depth and a shallow personality. If someone is obsessed with taking selfies it is most likely because the individual is self-absorbed and narcissistic.

A recurring tweet says it all, albeit with delicious irony: Never before has a generation so diligently recorded themselves accomplishing so little.

GLOBALISATION

> Today, no country can ever truly cut itself off from the global media or from external sources of information; trends that start in one corner of the world are rapidly replicated thousands of miles away.... A country trying to opt out of the global economy by cutting itself off from external trade and capital flows will still have to deal with the fact that the expectations of its population are shaped by their awareness of living standards and cultural products emerging from the outside world.
> — Francis Fukuyama (1999)

Globalisation is the process whereby the world has become interconnected and certain organizations (especially businesses) and cultures have gained immense international influence. The world is now a global village. Anthony Giddens, Director of the London School of Economics, defines globalization as 'the intensification of worldwide social relations which link distant localities in such a way that local happenings are shaped by events occurring many miles away and vice versa.' (Steger, 2003) A terrorist filming a propaganda video in the remote mountains of Afghanistan causes consternation in New York, London and Sydney when his video is uploaded to YouTube and watched by millions of viewers around the world. Virtually every major meeting of global institutions like the International Monetary Fund, the World Bank and the World Trade Organization, results in protests around the world. Cartoons of Muhammad published in a Danish newspaper spark off riots in Karachi and Khartoum.

Highly sophisticated communication and information technology, affordable access to air travel, global news networks, mass immigration, social media, and the rise of multinational corporations have contributed to the contested phenomenon of globalisation. Cultures are no longer localised but spread across the world as people relocate or migrate. Those disillusioned with their own cultures explore other cultures. Ideologies and religious beliefs are distributed — even exported for popular consumption. Cultures are fused and confused and new cultures emerge as people pick and mix elements from different cultures to suit themselves. Digital worlds like Second Life or the Enterprise become sealed cocoons of self-contained cultures. Traditional cultures are abandoned and replaced by new customs and values.

For centuries, the West exported its Christian faith and morality to the world. There were, undoubtedly, mixed motives for the global missionary movement. What is problematic about the new globalization is the global export and mass consumption of contemporary Western values that have their roots in postmodernism, humanism, hedonism and consumerism.

Sexual promiscuity, homosexuality, pornography, abortion, euthanasia, drug abuse, and the get-rich-quick dream are the ideals and values that are practised and promoted globally. The new global icons are those of Apple, Coca Cola, McDonald's, and Nike. Western celebrities like the Kardashians and Justin Bieber and talk show hosts like Oprah Winfrey are idolised across continents. Cultural narratives are controlled and created by large corporations, Hollywood and secular Western governments and even search engines like Google.

Christian values are not only rejected but seen as backward, harmful and, in some countries, illegal. In 2016, a report of a conference convened by an executive agency of the UK Foreign and Commonwealth Office argued that Evangelical Christians in the 'Global South' (often called the developing world) should be expected to 'reinterpret' the Bible to make it compatible with lesbian, gay, bi-sexual and transgender (LGBT) ideology. The recommendations, if implemented, would massively reverse freedom of religion across the globe. Barnabas Fund, an international charity supporting persecuted Christians all over the world, took a bold stand in exposing this pernicious globalising agenda.

Some believe that globalisation is beneficial because it creates a unified humanity. However, in some instances it is doing the exact opposite as religions, cultures and ethnic groups polarise themselves in an effort to resist the influence of globalisation and so protect their ways of life.

> ... modern technological change and scientific discoveries, particularly those that promote increasing communications between people in very diverse cultures, will very likely result in continuing, and possibly escalating, conflict and chaos over the decades to come. (Jenner, 2010)

EXISTENTIALISM

> There is something infantile in the presumption that somebody else has a responsibility to give your life meaning and point.... The truly adult view, by contrast, is that our life is as meaningful, as full and as wonderful as we choose to make it — Richard Dawkins, *The God Delusion* (2006)

Existentialism is a worldview that emphasizes defining self and the meaning of life through free will and choice. Choices are based on personal beliefs which existentialists themselves construct, based on what is appealing, suitable or convenient at the time. Choices are made without reference to objective truth, tested tradition, or a higher power. Existentialism is by definition amoral — not guided by a moral code.

As the meaning of life is self-constructed, a significant emphasis is placed on personal experiences and emotions. Instant gratification is important because existentialists live in the here and now.

People in an existential society are less likely to offer themselves for any form of service for fear of giving up control over themselves or their lives. This reduces their involvement in civic life and their participation in altruistic activities.

Another result of existentialism is a transient workforce who are in a job for only a very limited time. 'Job hopping is the new normal,' claims a Forbes report. Ninety-one percent of people born after 1985 stay in a job for less than three years, primarily, they say, because they do not want other people to control them. 'Paying one's dues, earning respect and promotion through service, commitment, dedication and self-sacrifice are no longer considered important. Instead finding a work environment that is conducive to a good and instantly gratifying experience and lifestyle is considered vital. Despite working for a company, individuals tend not to consider themselves as employees but as free agents.' (Meister, 2012)

Existentialism has especially influenced the education system in the West. It increasingly privileges subjective experience over objective truth. A British teacher-training textbook for pre-school childhood development drills teachers in the practical outworking of this philosophy.

> The teacher in existentialist education is there to provide pathways for students to explore their own values, meanings, and choices. In order to do this, learners need to be aware of as many options and choices as possible; they need to feel empowered and free to determine their own values and identities; and they need a multiplicity of experiences to enhance their self-awareness. The teacher's primary responsibility is to provide all these things, and to maintain a learning environment where students feel encouraged to express themselves through discussion, creative projects, and choice of study areas.

The role of the student is to determine their own values and identity. Freedom, choice, and responsibility form a complex interrelation in existentialist philosophy. The student is free to form and pursue their own values, but that freedom comes includes taking full responsibility for those values. The existentialist student accepts responsibility for their own values, feelings, and actions, because these have been self-generated rather than dictated by an authority. The Constructivist Classroom and Curriculum (2012)

Very few, however, recognize their ideological captivity to existentialism. Most people are existentialists and live existential lives without realising it. Some scholars even call it radical individualism as it involves a complete focus on self.

INDIFFERENCE

It might seem easy to predict that [faith] would become irrelevant in the age of smartphones, but this is part of a larger trend. Around the world, when asked about their feelings on religion, more and more people are responding with a "meh."
— Gabe Bullard (2016)

There is a growing trend of ambivalence and indifference, not just to religion, but also to the world and to life itself amongst millennials. The expressions 'meh' or 'whatever' — popular among millennials — reflect this complete lack of interest. 'Most religious communities' central problem is not teenage rebellion but teenagers' benign "whateverism,"' observes sociologist Christian Smith.

Gallup compiled the results of more than 30 studies involving over a million millennials in the US work force. The study revealed that 71% of millennials were disengaged or uninterested at work. More than half were planning to leave their jobs within the next year. Millennials were in need of constant praise and encouragement, more than any other generation. Seventy-two percent were unable to take initiative, lacked focus and needed additional direction in establishing task priorities compared with any other age group. This is alarming, as millennials will make up over than three-quarters of the work force by 2025. (Rigoni & Nelson, 2016)

This generation is less politically or religiously active or involved than any other generation in modern times. A study by Twenge, Freeman and Campbell compared attitudes and actions of high school and college students in the USA over 43 years. It concluded that millennials are more socially, civically and politically disengaged than any generation since the Second World War. More than 75% of millennials said that wealth was one of their primary motivators in life. Of all the factors measured, civic engagement, interest in 'social capital' and concern for others were the lowest of any generation since the 1940s. The study cited a number of possible influences including media, education, individualism, materialism and a 'generation me' culture as the main causes of this disengagement. They found there was more of an emphasis on extrinsic values such as money, fame, and image, and less emphasis on intrinsic values such as self-acceptance, group affiliation and community.

Another American study of millennials revealed their apathy about religion.

They're also the least religious generation in history — they're even getting less religious as they get older, which is unprecedented — and the majority of them identify Christianity as synonymous with harsh political conservatism. As older, more religious generations fade away and younger generations replace them, the societal midpoint shifts. And this trend is going to accelerate in coming years, because the millennial generation is big. They're even bigger than the baby boomers. (Lee, 2014)

Millennials tend to avoid anything that makes them feel uncomfortable. Students at a number of prestigious universities in the UK and the US are now demanding 'safe spaces,' censoring free speech that might cause offence and disinviting or no-platforming speakers who hold a conservative worldview. In the last couple of years, standard dictionaries have included the noun 'snowflake generation' in their vocabulary. Collins Dictionary defines it as 'the generation of people who became adults in the 2010s, viewed as being less resilient and more prone to taking offence than previous generations.' The Cambridge Dictionary characterizes it as 'a way of referring to the type of young people who are considered by some people to be too easily upset and offended.'

'...it is important to note that young people who cry offence are not feigning hurt — generational fragility is a real phenomenon,' notes Claire Fox, Director of the Institute of Ideas. 'By the time they get to university, our overprotected children are so loaded up with emotional angst that they are ill-equipped to deal with the basic challenges of adult life. The sad fact is that we are encouraging a whole generation to perceive itself as mentally ill,' she observes. Fox argues that the 'snowflake generation' phenomenon is the by-product of the health-and-safety mania that mollycoddles children, anti-bullying campaigns which pathologise normal childish transgressions and tensions, and the child-protection industry that actively encourages children to see potential abuse everywhere.

CULTURAL MARXISM

In 1923, a group of Marxist scholars founded the Institute of Social Research in Frankfurt. Two of the founders of the Frankfurt School, as it came to be known, were the Italian revolutionary Antonio Gramsci and the Hungarian radical György Lukács. Other Marxist academics like Wilhelm Reich, Theodor Adorno, Herbert Marcuse, Max Horkheimer, Erich Fromm, Jürgen Habermas and others joined them in a project that would alter the entire course of Western civilization.

Marx had tried to transform the traditional economic model of the West by instigating workers to revolt against the capitalists. However, with the outbreak of the First World War in 1914, when the workers of the world donned the uniforms of their countries and waged war against one another instead of revolting against their capitalist overlords, Marx's prophecy was proved false. The scholars of the Frankfurt School realized that the workers or proletariat could no longer be their target if they wanted to achieve a revolution that would fundamentally transform Western society. The working class had failed to carry out Marx's utopian dream. Now, they redirected their efforts at the cultural elite of society — the media, schools, universities, government, judiciary and even the churches — who were proud of Christianity and Western civilization. The enemy to be destroyed was the Christian-based civilisation of the West. 'Who was to save us from Western civilisation?' asked Lukács.

The tool to achieve this destruction was Critical Theory. Every aspect of Western culture had to be undermined by incessant and unrelenting criticism. The West had to be portrayed as evil, corrupt, authoritarian and oppressive. Christianity, capitalism, authority, family, patriotism, patriarchy, morality, and especially traditional sexual morality had to be attacked and brought down. Marxism had cried out against the oppression of the workers. Cultural Marxism turned its attention to creating specific victim groups — women, homosexuals, racial and ethnic minorities, etc. They portrayed the oppressor as Western Christian civilisation, the traditional nuclear family, parents, the white heterosexual male, the Christian church, the capitalists and all conservative and traditional values.

The Nazis forced the leading lights of the Frankfurt School to flee from Germany — because most of them were Jews and all of them were Communists. These neo-Marxists escaped to the US, where a number of them joined the faculty of Columbia University and other prestigious universities like Princeton, Brandeis, and California at Berkeley. Instead of expressing gratitude for their newfound freedom, the cultural Marxists began to infiltrate the academy and inject their ideas into mainstream American culture.

The most important task for cultural Marxism was to 'capture the culture.' Marx had already declared a war on religion calling it the 'opiate of the masses.' In *The Communist Manifesto* in 1848, he declared war on the family. 'Abolition of the family! Even the most radical flare up at this infamous proposal of the Communists,' he wrote. The academics of the Frankfurt School triggered a revolution against the family by unleashing a new era of sexual permissiveness and promiscuity and setting out on 'the long march through the institutions,' thus achieving the vision of Antonio Gramsci.

Two texts, Reich's *The Sexual Revolution* and Marcuse's *Eros and Civilization*, were seminal works. For Reich, 'The patriarchal family is the structural and ideological breeding ground of all social orders based on the authoritarian principle.' Hence, it was vital to 'eliminate the sexual repressions and dissolve the infantile ties to the parents.' Gabriele Kuby explains how 'Reich recognized that total sexualisation of the culture would mean extermination of the churches and the traditional state, and this was his goal.' Marcuse advocated what he called 'polymorphous perversity' which encouraged sexual gratification outside the conventional channels of accepted sexual behaviour and permitted almost any means that allowed for gratification, including stimulation from or intercourse with the same sex.

Cultural Marxism was also responsible for the introduction of political correctness. Marcuse argued that, because Western society was inherently oppressive, a tolerance for all viewpoints actually contributed to social oppression. Hence, there would have to be 'repressive tolerance' or an outright 'intolerance against movements from the Right and toleration of movements from the Left.' Because society is unequal we should not treat all ideas as equal and hence we should be intolerant and repressive in the name of tolerance and liberty. This doctrine is at the heart of the new intolerance against Christians or conservatives speaking for Biblical and traditional values.

Cultural Marxism, better known as Leftism, is one of the greatest threats to Christianity, Western civilization and freedom today. It is a totalitarian movement seeking a new world order through a 'cultural revolution ... taking place behind people's backs—top-down. It emanates from the power elites and is propelled by minorities who define themselves by sexual orientation and seek to topple the world order. Indeed, a change in values can only lead to a change in the world order. Because the changes are global, it is to be expected that the development aims at a new global order,' writes Kuby.

In the next chapter we will explore just how much Western culture has influenced the Church and how the Church can respond to Western culture.

3

HOW THE CHURCH HAS BEEN INFLUENCED BY WESTERN CULTURE: MORALITY AND MATERIALISM

I believe that one reason why the church of God at this present moment has so little influence over the world is because the world has so much influence over the church. Nowadays we have Nonconformists pleading that they may do this and they may do that — things which their Puritan forefathers would rather have died at the stake than have tolerated. They plead that they may live like worldlings, and my sad answer to this, when they crave for this liberty is, "Do it if you dare. It may not do you much hurt, for you are so bad already. Your cravings show how rotten your hearts are. If you have a hungering after such dog's meat, go, dogs, and eat the garbage. Worldly amusements are fit food for mere pretenders and hypocrites. If you were God's children you would loathe the very thought of the world's evil joys, and your question would not be, 'how far may we be like the world?' but your one cry would be, 'How much can we come out of it?'" — C. H. Spurgeon (1886)

The tidal waves of Western culture and the new civic religion of humanism have lashed the Church, causing chaos and inflicting irreparable damage. There are, of course, small bastions of believers in the West who remain faithful. However, it would be rare to find a church or a Christian immune to any influence from the onslaught of contemporary culture.

CHRISTIAN MORALITY AND BEHAVIOUR

But just as he who called you is holy, so be holy in all you do; for it is written: 'Be holy, because I am holy.' (1 Peter 1:15-16)

To be holy is to be set apart. Eugene Peterson in *The Message* paints a vibrant portrait of holy living in his translation. 'As obedient children, let yourselves be pulled into a way of life shaped by God's life, a life energetic and blazing with holiness. God said, "I am holy; you be holy."' It should be easy for non-Christians to recognise Christians by the way we live. Regrettably, study after study confirms that there is little to distinguish the behaviour and lifestyle of Christians in the West from non-Christians around them.

It is also notable that Biblical Christian discipline within churches is becoming increasingly rare. The church has largely abdicated responsibility for church discipline and passed it instead to the State. Christians are increasingly turning to the police and the law courts to resolve their internal disputes and to fulfil their objectives.

Divorce

In 2008, the Barna Group compared the divorce rates of 'born again Christians' with the national average in the US. The researchers categorised their subjects into 'born again' or 'not born again' depending on information shared by each person about their spiritual life.

Their results sent shock waves through the Christian community. 'Born again Christians' were more likely to divorce than the national average. The divorce rate amongst Christians was 27% compared to the national average of 25%. Atheists and agnostics had the lowest divorce rate at 21%. Christians belonging to independent churches had an even higher divorce rate of 34%. Mainline denominations registered slightly lower divorce rates, but they were still higher than the national average with Methodists at 26%, Episcopalians and Pentecostals at 28%, and Baptists at 29%. Only Lutherans (21%) and Presbyterians (23%) registered lower than average rates.

Responding to the study, George Barna, founder of the Barna Group, said that 'of more than 70 other moral behaviours we study, when we compare Christians to non-Christians we rarely find substantial differences.'

Self-Indulgence
In an earlier study, Barna found that Christians are as likely to engage in immoral and sinful patterns and self-oriented behaviours that benefit themselves and were more self-indulgent and self-gratifying than non-Christians.

The study entitled *American Lifestyles Mix Compassion and Self-Oriented Behaviour* surveyed behaviours and activities like helping the poor, volunteering, lying, violence, spousal abuse, swearing, revengeful acts, stealing, pornography, care for the environment, adultery, gambling, alcoholism, drug abuse and consulting a psychic or medium for guidance and found no statistically significant difference between Christians and non-Christians. The only substantial differences found were that Christians were less likely to recycle, more likely to volunteer at their churches and less likely to download music illegally. They were also less likely to view sexually explicit movies and magazines, to use profanity in public, or to buy a lottery ticket, though the difference in these cases from non-born again adults was too small to be statistically significant.

Litigation
Christians are just as likely to sue as non-Christians, often bringing cases against other Christians. They appear just as willing to fight for

their personal interests and chase compensation for perceived wrongs, offenses and defamations. According to Peacemaker Ministries, 'born again Christians in the US file 4 to 8 million lawsuits every year, often against other Christians, costing 20 to 40 billion dollars.' (Sande, 2015)

Sexual Behaviour

Research shows that evangelical teenagers are likely to be more sexually immoral than their non-Christian peers. Christian teens in the US tend to have their first full sexual encounter at a younger age (average 16.3 years) than non-Christians (average 16.7 years). Young Christians are far more likely to have had three or more sexual partners (13.7%) than non-Christians (8.9%). Mark Regnerus blames the prevailing Western culture and the American school system which encourages and promotes moral relativism. (Regnerus, 2007)

In 2007, *World Magazine* revealed that 80% of Christian young adults (aged 18 to 29) confessed to having premarital sex, compared to the national average of 88%. Of the 80%, 64% said they had engaged in premarital sex in the past year and 42% said they were in a current sexual relationship outside marriage. In the US, 30% of unmarried Christian women between the ages of 18-29 became pregnant. This is one percent higher than non-Christians.

A study by Strayhorn and Strayhorn (2009) on unplanned pregnancies of unmarried American teenagers found a direct correlation between religiosity (defined as 'evangelical and born-again') and unplanned premarital pregnancies — the more Christian a community, the greater the chance of teenage pregnancies in that community. Although hesitant to draw causal conclusions, the researchers suggest that the high rate of pregnancies amongst Christian teens, compared to non-Christian teens, was because of the Christians' relative lack of sex education and contraception use. 'Nonetheless,' they report, 'the magnitude of the correlation between religiosity and teen birth rate astonished us.'

Gene Veith, author of *Sex and the Evangelical Teen* (2007), lays the blame not only on the prevailing culture in Western society, but also on the prevailing culture in the Church.

> It goes deeper than that. Churches used to teach and exemplify self-control, the necessity of keeping one's emotions in check, the discipline of self-denial and mortification of the flesh. Today the typical evangelical church, in its example and practice, cultivates "letting go," emotionalism, self-fulfilment, and an odd religious sensuality.

It appears that the current church culture, although not expressly promoting such behaviour, is unwittingly creating an environment where such behaviour is inevitable. Professor Scot McKnight comments on the role of the evolving culture within the Church.

> As young Christians mature into their 20s, it's natural for them to re-evaluate their beliefs as they strive to figure out how faith fits into their expanding worldview. If they determine they can drink responsibly and watch movies and listen to music with a discerning spirit, is it possible the "don't do it because it's wrong" message gets tossed aside along with all those other "legalistic" messages of youth? That they start to believe they can also have sex "with discernment." — cited in *Relevant Magazine* (September/October 2011)

Paradoxically, a study by Ellison Research revealed that 87% of Americans believe in the concept of sin. The study defined sin as 'something that is almost always considered wrong from a religious or moral perspective.' However, the survey demonstrates a marked lack of consensus as to what actions or lifestyles came under this definition. While 81% of Americans consider adultery a sin, only 46% felt sex before marriage was sinful and only 29% felt lying was a sin. 'A lot of this is relative,' the study concluded. 'We tend to view sin not as God views it, but how we view it.' (Ron Sellers, Ellison president 2008).

Pastor-theologian Tim Keller points out how the word 'sin' has essentially been 'rebranded.' 'I use it with lots and lots of explanation because the word is essentially obsolete,' he says. Western culture has influenced the Church to such an extent that it has relativized the concept of sin completely. Sin is now whatever an individual interprets it to be, irrespective of Holy Scripture.

'If we claim to be without sin, we deceive ourselves,' warns the apostle John (1 John 1:8). Many Western Christians, through choice or ignorance, are unaware of sin in their lives. Not surprisingly, the prayer of confession, which was an indispensable part of the liturgy for centuries, has now been dumbed down with new verbal formulae that may not even contain the words 'sin' or 'confess.'

Peter Mullen, former Chaplain to the London Stock Exchange, points to the *Idiot's Guide to Common Worship* produced by the Archbishop's Council of the Church of England where 'Confession' is retitled 'Doing the dirt on ourselves.' Columnist Peter Hitchens laments the demise of Thomas Cranmer's *Book of Common Prayer* (1662), particularly for its robust treatment of sin. 'The Prayer Book has another striking feature,' he notes. 'It demands penitence as the price of entry to all its ceremonies. The hard passage from the First Epistle of John — "If we say that we have no sin, we deceive ourselves, and the truth is not in us" — is often the first thing spoken. Soon afterward, the general confession requires a public declaration that "We have erred, and strayed from thy ways like lost sheep." There is "no health in us." We are "miserable offenders." These are not easy words to say, if you mean them.... The fact is, many people prefer not to say them, because they do not like to admit that this is so. The church's solution to this unpopularity was to abandon the requirement, replacing it with vague, half-hearted mumblings or — more often — with nothing at all,' he laments.

The problem is compounded by a general reluctance of preachers to address the topic of sin in church. Sin is rarely the focus of sermons or Bible teaching. This could be a reaction to the 'turn or burn' sermons of fanatical groups, a flawed grasp of the theology of holiness and grace, an effort not to offend people in a postmodern society or an attempt to be 'seeker sensitive' by luring potential converts with an appealing message.

It is also possible that church leaders reluctant to preach on sin are themselves compromised by a sinful lifestyle. Internet pornography is a constant struggle, confessed 37% of pastors in the US, in research carried out by *Christianity Today* in 2001. Whatever the reason, the church's silence implicitly endorses sinful behaviour among Christians.

Few studies have been carried out on the distinction between Christian and non-Christian moral behaviour in other Western countries besides the US. According to the Pew Study on the Global Views on Morality (2013), the US is more conservative than any other Western country (and leading by a considerable margin). For example, 30% of the country consider premarital sex unacceptable moral behaviour compared to Australia (15%), Canada (15%), Britain (13%), Germany (6%) and France (6%). Almost half of all Americans (49%) believe that abortion is wrong, while only 26% of Australians and Canadians, 25% of Britons, 19% of Germans and 14% of the French believe it is immoral. Americans are dramatically more conservative on moral issues like adultery, homosexuality, alcoholism and divorce than their counterparts in Europe. The question is whether this ideological conservatism actually translates into daily moral behaviour and lifestyle.

A New Morality
Is morality declining or is it developing? Edward L. Rubin, in *Soul, Self and Society: The New Morality and the Modern State* (2015) rejects the pessimistic claim that morality is in decline. 'People who think morality is declining or disappearing have really just failed to adjust to this huge change in the way many people in Western civilization look at the world,' he argues. Rubin, who is Professor of Political Science and Law at Vanderbilt University, sees a new emerging form of morality, which should be encouraged and promoted. 'The new morality is based on concepts of self-fulfilment. You're supposed to live the best life you possibly can for yourself, and there's essentially nothing beyond the experience of life that justifies it.... Self-fulfilment is a real morality....' He contrasts the new morality with traditional Christian morality and

calls for Christianity to adapt itself to the new morality. 'As the morality of self-fulfilment becomes dominant, Christianity may be reinterpreted once more, in a manner that is largely consistent with the new morality. The other possibility is that it will decay. The new morality already encourages people to shop for the denomination that best fulfils their spiritual needs. In the future, they may shop among the entire range of world religions and philosophies.' (Rubin, 2015)

The new morality of self-fulfilment is rife in the Western church and is reflected in the materialism and consumerism practised by Western Christians.

MATERIALISM AND CONSUMERISM

So what is the difference between someone who wilfully indulges in sexual pleasures while ignoring the Bible on moral purity and someone who wilfully indulges in the selfish pursuit of more and more material possessions while ignoring the Bible on caring for the poor? The difference is that one involves a social taboo in the church and the other involves the social norm in the church.— David Platt (2010)

In 2011, researchers at Bath University conducted a study into the buying habits of British Christians. Even though Christians in the sample group agreed that materialism was wrong, their buying habits did not reflect this belief. Christians were willing to acquire material goods if convinced of a product's functional value. Christian spending was very similar to that of non-Christians. While Christians used a number of reasons to justify their extravagant and superfluous purchases and 'ignore core beliefs,' they admitted that the underlying and probably unconscious reason for purchases was materialism. The authors of this secular study were surprised by the results since they expected Christians to be less inclined to purchase goods which were expensive, luxury and even unnecessary. They concluded that the study 'may help to explain how Christians acquire and store material items for themselves and their family, despite many biblical teachings that discourage hoarding wealth.'

Materialism and consumerism are perhaps the most subtle yet destructive influences that Western culture has had on Christians. The church not only accepts the culture of materialism and consumerism, it actively promotes it as virtuous. Obviously, the church does not name such 'isms' but re-brands them with euphemisms and buzz phrases baptised with pseudo-Christian content. It touts the merits of being 'culturally relevant,' 'seeker sensitive,' and 'living in a different context.' The Gospel of a 'God without wrath, who brought men without sin, into a kingdom without judgement, through the ministrations of a Christ without a Cross,' — in Niebuhr's phrase — is designed, packaged and marketed to appeal to a target group of consumers. Andrew Walker laments how a consumerist culture in Church has turned 'ascetic individualism' (doing good) based on severe self-discipline, self-sacrifice and self-denial, into 'hedonistic individualism' (feeling good) based on self-interest, self-importance and instant gratification.

A consumerist culture supplants existing culture when the consumer habits of individuals begin to shape and define its values, morals, norms and behaviour. As consumers shape Western culture, so do consumer Christians shape the church, observes Shiao Chong in *Have it Your Way? When the Church Embraces Consumerism*. Chong identifies the three core values of consumerism: individual choice is supreme, the customer is boss and the consumer's wants cannot be allowed to be fully satisfied.

Individual Choice is Supreme

Christian consumers no longer regard doctrine as the core criterion for choosing a church. Instead, many Christians now 'shop around' for churches that support their self-indulgent lifestyles, life-choices, personal views and beliefs about God. If a church challenges their opinions and behaviour, consumerist Christians are quick to take offence, voice their dissatisfaction and exercise their individual choice by shopping for another church that meets their expectations.

The Customer is Boss

Churches respond by adopting the 'customer is boss' mantra. Church leaders design services and programmes to meeting the needs, or, more accurately, the wants, of the consumer Christian. Services become sensationalist, experiential and entertaining. Church buildings strive to be bigger, brighter and model themselves on entertainment venues. Preaching is therapeutic and motivational, tiptoeing around challenging or controversial issues. Attendees recommend the church based on how much they enjoyed the service what they got out of it. Nigel Scotland highlights the customer mentality in *Shopping for a Church: Consumerism and the Churches.*

> Christians do not endorse prosperity theology, they have nevertheless taken on board much of its consumer worldview. Thus the starting point of many has become my needs, my self-interest and my satisfaction. Much of contemporary evangelism tells people Jesus will make them happy and fulfilled. People therefore look for a church that meets their needs and they go to worship for what they can get out of it. Indeed the comment 'I didn't get much out of that service' is often passed without even a thought that there might have to be a sacrifice of praise and thanksgiving or a concerted effort to worship God with all of one's heart, mind, soul and strength. Thus for many churchgoers Christianity has become primarily a lifestyle, an ethos, a culture or a club, rather than a faith or relationship with a Lord who demands total commitment on the part of his followers and who wants them to live in community relationships with others.

Imperative to the church's survival is the showmanship of preachers, worship leaders and worship bands. The mega-church, the coffee-shop centred church, the celebrity pastor and the trendy and hip worship leader are seen as marks of a church's success. But such a Christian consumerist culture does not really meet the deepest needs of hurting persons, as this heart-rending appeal made by a young widow, whose husband died after a two-year battle with cancer illustrates.

I am not paying attention to the church décor when I walk through the doors. I don't want to smell fresh brewed coffee in the lobby. I don't want to see a trendy pastor on the platform. I don't care about the graphics or the props on the platform. I am hurting in a way that is almost indescribable. My days are spent working full time. My nights are spent home schooling and taking care of two young children. And when I go to church I desperately want to hear the Word of God. Because there are days I am running on empty and a coffee bar in the lobby isn't filling me up. There are days when the pain is so brutal and a concert like setting is not providing healing. There are days when the tears won't stop and a trendsetting church is not what I need. I need Jesus. There are days I wonder if the pain is ever going to end and a couch on the platform is not providing answers. The lighting, coffee bars, relevant messages, graphics and other things are secondary and serve no assistance to me during the darkest hour of my life. (Lira, 2017)

The Consumer's Wants Cannot Be Allowed to be Fully Satisfied
Consumerist churches make sure that their customers are never fully satisfied. They want their customers to continue to consume. They create even more needs and claim to offer solutions to these needs. As in fashion magazines, they make Christian consumers feel inadequate or unfulfilled in their spiritual and physical lives guaranteeing success in life and deliverance from all that is bad. If only their customers will abide by a certain model, buy a self-help book, attend a seminar or conference, join a programme, latch on to the latest trend, or invest their offerings in a spiritual scheme, they will be healthy, wealthy and fulfilled.

The Biblical prophets were intent on turning people away from sin and pointing them towards God. They spoke 'truth to power' in messages that were terrifying, challenging and offensive — to such a degree, that they were often killed for proclaiming the truth. The prophetic paradigm has been turned on its head with Christians seeking false prophets who will comfort them with revelations of success, blessing and happiness.

The chief desire of the Protestant Reformers was to equip ordinary people to read and interpret the Bible for themselves. 'If God spare my life, before very long I shall cause a plough boy to know the scriptures better than you do!' the 16th century English reformer William Tyndale responded heatedly to an Anglican priest. Five hundred years after Martin Luther nailed his 95 Theses to a church door in Wittenberg, consumerist Christianity has turned the Reformation upside down.

Now, a new breed of 'anointed' pastors and prophets claim insights into hidden truths of the Bible that are revealed exclusively to them. This has given rise to a steady growth of independent churches which according to CNN (The Rise of Evangelical "Nones," 2015) is the fastest growing church group in the US. There are, undoubtedly, many theologically sound independent churches and the factors surrounding the growth of independent churches is multi-faceted. Nevertheless, there is every reason to believe that tailoring doctrine and practice to suit Christian niche markets is one of the primary factors giving rise to many independent churches. Nigel Scotland calls this 'privatising church,' which he attributes to a 'rampant' individualism and consumerism within the church.

Ignoring completely the supreme model of Jesus, who 'though he was rich, yet for your sake he became poor' (2 Corinthians 8:9) and 'made himself nothing by taking the very nature of a servant' (Philippians 2:7), consumer Christians follow the model of celebrity preachers who own private jets, huge estates and are worth millions of dollars. Their 'health and wealth' Gospel married to an obscenely opulent lifestyle, has further promoted a culture of consumerism within the Church.

Health and Wealth Gospel
The 'health and wealth' Gospel endorses material success and well-being as a sign of God's blessing and favour. Conversely, if a Christian faces sickness, failure, poverty and persecution, this is considered an indicator of lacking God's favour or a lack of the believer's faith. Tragically, some Christians in the West assume that their material abundance is evidence of God's approval of them and their country, in contrast to God's displeasure at poor individuals and poor countries.

They end up feeling spiritually superior to those facing practical difficulties and privations. The 'health and wealth as sign of spiritual success' doctrine is widely exported across the world through mission trips, mass outreaches, books, the internet and so-called Christian television. The poor in the West or in developing countries are made to feel inadequate, inferior, abandoned and unloved by God because of their poverty. Shockingly, this amounts to a form of imperialism based on a consumerist culture. Churches are planted in the image of the 'successful' Western church model, and pastors and Christians in non-Western contexts are taught to emulate the Western Church model.

The Gospel as Moralistic Therapeutic Deism
After conducting extensive research among Christian youth in the US, sociologists Christian Smith and Melinda Lundquist Denton concluded that 'the *de facto* dominant religion among contemporary teenagers in the United States is what we might call "Moralistic Therapeutic Deism."' Smith and Denton outline the creed of this religion as follows:

1. There is a God who created the world and watches over us.

2. God wants people to be good, nice, and fair to each other, as taught in the Bible and by most world religions.

3. The central goal of life is to be happy and to feel good about oneself.

4. God does not need to be particularly involved in one's life except when he is needed to resolve a problem.

5. Good people go to heaven when they die.

'...Moralistic Therapeutic Deism is about inculcating a moralistic approach to life. It believes that central to living a good and happy life is being a good, moral person. That means being nice, kind, pleasant, respectful, and responsible; working on self-improvement; taking care of one's health; and doing one's best to be successful. ... Feeling good about oneself is thus also an essential aspect of living a moral life, according to this dominant *de facto* teenage religious faith.' Smith and Denton elaborate: 'Moralistic Therapeutic Deism is also about providing therapeutic benefits to its adherents. This is not a religion of repentance from sin, of keeping the Sabbath, of living as a servant of a sovereign divine, of steadfastly saying one's prayers, of faithfully observing high holy days, of building character through suffering, of basking in God's love and grace, of spending oneself in gratitude and love for the cause of social justice, etc. Rather, what appears to be the actual dominant religion among U.S. teenagers is centrally about feeling good, happy, secure, at peace. It is about attaining subjective well-being, being able to resolve problems, and getting along amiably with other people.'

In his letter to the Galatians, the apostle Paul warned Christians to beware of 'another gospel.' This new-fangled, trendy gospel was infiltrating the church in Galatia. It was so persuasive and so pervasive, its false teaching was seducing even Christians. 'I am astonished that you are so quickly deserting the one who called you by the grace of Christ and are turning to a different gospel,' writes Paul (Galatians 1:6). Paul's implication is clear. There is only one Gospel. There cannot be another Gospel. Another gospel is always a fake, bogus and spurious gospel. Anyone who rejects the Gospel of Jesus and settles for another gospel is in effect rejecting Jesus as Lord and in doing so rejecting God himself.

In this chapter, we saw how the Western church has fallen prey to immorality and the false gospel of consumerism and materialism thus endangering its spirituality. In the next chapter, we will consider the impact of modern Western culture on the core Christian activities of service to the poor, mission and evangelism, and congregational worship.

4

HOW THE CHURCH HAS BEEN INFLUENCED BY WESTERN CULTURE: SERVICE AND WORSHIP

And whatever you do, whether in word or deed, do it all in the name of the Lord Jesus, giving thanks to God the Father through him. (Colossians 3:17)

The word for 'work' and the word for 'worship' is the same word in the Hebrew Bible — the root verb *avad*. The noun for 'servant' or 'slave' — *eved* — is derived from this root, and is also the word used for 'worshipper.' In Egypt, the Israelites worked as slaves for Pharaoh. They could not worship their God. After the Exodus, God commanded the Israelites to worship Him. The Bible uses the same Hebrew word to describe the hard labour Pharaoh inflicted on the Israelite slaves and the joyful worship Yahweh required from the Israelite people. This is the reason many churches designate their Christian worship meeting as a 'Service.' It is also the reason Christians refer to our good deeds of assistance, help and charity as 'service' or 'ministry.' Our motive for 'whatever we do,' then, is from our understanding that we do it for God and 'in the name of the Lord Jesus.'

CHRISTIAN SERVICE AND GIVING

Western culture has distorted the Biblical understanding of Christian service to the poor and needy, as taught by Jesus in His parable of the Good Samaritan.

Christians in the postmodern West are undoubtedly serving the poor and needy through acts of charity, mercy and justice. However, in many cases, they are performing acts of service not because of love of neighbour or obedience to Jesus, but because of how it makes them feel.

In 2014, *Psychology Today* published an article entitled 'Helper's High: The Benefits (and risks) of Altruism.' It suggested that altruism is rarely selfless and that people are volunteering to help others not because of the good act or the need but because of the effects on the helper. 'Research suggests that helpers may gain more from their altruistic acts than recipients.' Helping others releases endorphins, creates a feeling of satisfaction, helps one feel more grateful for what one has, distracts helpers from their own problems and improves physical health, they conclude. Doing good is thus focused on the helper, rather than the person in need.

In both cases, the helper does good and helps the needy. Nevertheless, there is a subtle difference. The primary motive is the wellbeing of self rather than obedience to Jesus and the imitation of His selfless service. We should not feel guilty about experiencing feelings of wellbeing when helping others, but we must be honest with ourselves about our possibly mixed motives.

Many acts of service require sacrifice and humility. They are hard, time consuming, tiring, dangerous and dirty. Would we still help if the task was difficult, dirty, and created no emotional high? Would we do good for goodness' sake and for Christ's sake? Would we serve if it did not make us feel good, or if our service was thankless and received neither attention nor praise?

One of the greatest indictments on the church in the West is its attitude towards the poor. Christians in the West are mostly oblivious to the plight of the poor and persecuted.

A British study by the Church Urban Fund, entitled *Bias to the Poor? Christian Attitudes to Poverty in this Country* (2012), found that 'attending church appears to do little to change people's underlying attitudes to poverty and inequality, with no great differences between the views of churchgoers and non-churchgoers.' Both churchgoers and non-churchgoers displayed negative attitudes to the poor, attributing poverty to laziness, lack of will power and many saw it as an inevitable part of modern life. The study revealed that attitudes of British churchgoers towards the poor in the UK have become increasingly unsympathetic over the last 20 years.

While some of these attitudes may be attributed to the popular dissatisfaction with the welfare state and 'benefit scroungers' taking advantage of the system, it fails to explain why Christians gave less to charity than Muslims or Jews. In 2013, the *Huffington Post* reported that British Muslims give more to charity than any other religious group. On average, a Muslim gives £371 per year, a Jew gives £270, but a Christian gives only £178, and an atheist gives £116 per year to charity.

The number of Christians contributing to the poor and to ministry is also diminishing. According to *Relevant Magazine* (Holmes, 2016), only 5% of Americans tithe regularly and those that do give an average of less than 2.5% per capita. Christian tithing has been on a steady decline in the US since the 1960s. Tithing was at its lowest in 2016 since the Great Depression in 1921, when it was 3.3%, Empty Tomb's report revealed. More serious is the accusation that American churches spend only a small portion of their money on the poor. Only 15% of the tithe is spent outside the church. The study found that churches are spending more on themselves to make their congregations comfortable. 'If a church is turning inward and valuing the happiness of its members over service to others, it is moving on a spectrum toward pagan values,' it warned.

At no time in the history of the church has so much been spent on satisfying the needs of rich believers while ignoring the plight of the poor. In a scathing indictment of the American church, sociologists Christian Smith and Michael Emerson attempt to solve 'the riddle of stingy Christian giving.' In their meticulously researched book *Passing the Plate: Why American Christians Don't Give Away More Money*, they write: 'American Christians are amongst the wealthiest of their faith in the world today and probably the most affluent single group of Christians in two thousand years of church history.... And yet, despite all of this, American Christians give away relatively little money to religious and other purposes. A sizeable number of Christians give no money, literally nothing. Most of the rest of American Christians give little sums of money. Only a small percentage of American Christians give money generously, in proportion to what their churches call them to give. All the evidence, we will see, points to the same conclusion: when it comes to sharing their money, most contemporary American Christians are remarkably ungenerous.'

Churches in the US spend over $35 billion a year on themselves. All over the West, the church spends money on buildings, soft chairs, coffee shops, sound and light equipment, even smoke machines. Meanwhile 2.4 billion people in the world live on less than $2 per day, few have sufficient food, water or shelter and many die of preventable diseases. Many of these are Christians who not only live in extreme poverty, but suffer persecution for their faith. An estimated 10% of all Christians live in contexts of anti-Christian discrimination, harassment or persecution.

There are complex reasons underlying the giving habits of Christians in the West. It may come down to a perception of who is poor. Many Western Christians are ignorant of the needs of their fellow-Christians in the non-Western world and place their own needs and wellbeing before the needs of the global church. While reading the story of the rich young ruler in Luke 18, Christians in the West may be reluctant to identify with the rich man, assuming that they themselves are not rich. Many Westerners would be shocked to know just how rich they are compared to the vast majority of the world's population. As David Platt points out:

• A person with assets of more than $2200 (US dollars) is richer than half the world's population.

• A person earning over $1500 per year is in the top 20% of the world richest.

• A person who has enough food, clothes, shelter and their own means of transport is in the top 15%.

• A person earning over $25,000 per year is in the top 10%.

• A person who has savings, a hobby that requires equipment or supplies, a variety of clothes in the cupboard, two cars (in any condition), and lives in their own home, is in the top 5% of the world's wealthy.

• A person earning over $50,000 annually is in the top 1% of the world's income earners.

Despite their own perceptions, the vast majority of Western Christians are rich. So why are most American Christians, who fit the above profile of rich people, so reluctant to give? Among other reasons, Smith and Emerson attribute this lack of generosity to the 'larger context of a massive economy, powerful culture, and ubiquitous advertising and media industries that are driven by and dedicated to the promotion of mass consumption.' 'Materialistic consumption has become a nearly inescapable way of life in the United States. In fact, American religion itself seems to be increasingly drawn into this consumerist mentality. Therefore, every Christian impulse to generously give money away inevitably runs up against potent counter-impulses driven by mass consumerism to instead perpetually spend, borrow, acquire, consume, discard, and then spend more on oneself and the family,' they write. American Christians seem to be also 'somewhat uninformed or confused about the meanings, expectations, and purposes of faithful Christian giving,' they add.

Unless Western Christians turn from their ignorance, apathy and selfishness they stand in grave danger of the Lord's judgement.

CHRISTIAN MISSION

John Paton (1824-1907) was a Scottish missionary who took the Gospel to the cannibals of the New Hebrides, now Vanuatu. Within weeks of arriving in the New Hebrides, his first wife and child died. He dug their graves with his bare hands. Four more children from his second marriage died in infancy on the mission field. Today, Vanuatu is 83% Christian, largely because of his missionary endeavours. Paton wrote:

> Trials and hairbreadth escapes only strengthened my faith and nerved me for more to follow; and they trod swiftly enough upon each other's heels. Without that abiding consciousness of the presence and power of my Lord and Saviour, nothing in the world could have preserved me from losing my reason and perishing miserably. His words 'Lo, I am with you always, even unto the end' became to me so real that it would not have startled me to behold Him, as Stephen did, gazing down upon the scene. It is the sober truth that I had my nearest and most intimate glimpses of the presence of my Lord in those dread moments when musket, club or spear was being levelled at my life.

Until the 1950s, missionaries were often 'one way' missionaries. They left for their mission field with a few meagre belongings, sometimes packed into their coffins, expecting never to return home. They gave up comfort, health and sometimes their own lives to spread the Gospel. They anticipated, faced and even welcomed great danger and trials.

They considered 'everything a loss because of the surpassing worth of knowing Christ Jesus, my Lord, for whose sake I have lost all things' (Philippians 3:8). They were following the example of the greatest missionary who ever lived and said, '...I have learned to be content whatever the circumstances. I know what it is to be in need, and I know what it is to have plenty. I have learned the secret of being content in any and every situation, whether well fed or hungry, whether living in plenty or in want' (Philippians 4:11-12). They knew 'that they were aliens and strangers on earth' and 'were longing for a better country — a heavenly one' (Hebrews 11:13,16). They were driven by an overwhelming and desperate love for God and for unsaved souls. Theirs was a lifelong calling.

Missionaries prepared themselves through fasting, prayer and in-depth study of God's Word. Many spent time learning medical and practical skills. When working in often hostile and dangerous places, they learned the language, customs and culture of the people they served. They not only built hospitals, schools, churches and orphanages but also forged long-term relationships with those they evangelised. This was possible only through years and even decades of service. Peter Milne, another missionary to the New Hebrides, died there after 50 years of service among head-hunters. When he died, the tribe he had dedicated most of his life to, buried him and inscribed these words on his tombstone:

'When he came there was no light. When he left there was no darkness.'

Contrast this with the explosion of short-term missions in today's Western Christian scenario. A short-term mission is a church or organisation sending a group of Western Christians to a developing world country for a brief stint of one to six weeks. Consider this advert on www.shorttermmissions.com invites applications for a short-term mission to the Bahamas.

What the Mission Trip Will Be Like

Arrive at the island and join the Bahamian people and culture as you continue to work with one of the most Christian nations (They still pray in school). The Bahamians are wonderfully spirited people.

The tropical beaches and ocean water is enchanting as you reach out and connect with the children, youth and families that are in need. You are in the right place for a calypso beat and a positive experience in sharing community! Expect a great time ... in the sun, and with the people of the Bahamas, as you meet the needs of others! We can arrange to take your team to one or more islands; minister and also allow some time for snorkelling and the beach – or stay with us on Grand Bahama island and work with our mission partners; we can house up to 45 people and hotels are available if you want an upgraded package.

Every year the Bahamas receives one short-term missionary for every 15 local residents. Given that over 96% of the population identify themselves as Christian, there is a short-term missionary for every individual non-Christian in the Bahamas. The short-term missionaries make little or no impact on the non-Christian population, as humanism, paganism and Islam have risen in recent years. Instead of preaching the Gospel, short-term missionaries paint schools, hand out food and have a holiday.

Contemporary Western culture has turned the model of one-way missionaries carrying their own coffins into the leisure activity of mission tourism that emphasizes comfort, new experiences, self-discovery, upgrades and risk-free adventure. There is little sacrifice apart from the expense of the trip.

Short-term missions are becoming increasingly popular. Over two million Christians from United States alone go on annual short-term missions, spending over four billion dollars each year.

God does not call every Christian to leave home and country to become long-term missionaries. God calls most of us to be witnesses where we are – local missionaries. Alas, many are reluctant to be witnesses either at home or abroad.

Promoters of short-term missions claim that these trips serve as an introduction to the global church, with those who have been short-term missionaries more likely to support the church and ministries in the developing world through prayer and giving, or even developing a vocation to long-term mission.

However, a quantitative study by Priest et al (2006) found that short-term missions actually have negative consequences for the long-term mission effort. They uncovered a negative correlation between the growing number of short-term missionaries and the declining number of long-term missionaries. Christians who had gone on a short-term mission felt that they had 'done their bit' and no longer need to consider whether God might be calling them to a far more sacrificial long-term mission.

What about the argument that short-term missionaries, having experienced the mission field, would be moved to support financially the global church and world mission on their return? Priest et al note that 'we were startled in our initial results, to discover that those who had never participated in STM [short-term missions] gave nearly three times as much on average to support [long-term] missionaries as those who had.' The evidence suggests that Christians who have been on short-term missions are more likely to spend money on themselves and their own experiences than on supporting missions or ministries. This is almost certainly a reflection of the impact of existentialism, individualism and materialism on millennials who are statistically the most likely to venture out on short-term missions.

More problematically, it appears that funding of short-term missions is diverting resources from long-term missions, further reducing the support for long-term missionaries. With the rise of independent churches, local congregations are more likely to spend their money supporting their own short-term mission teams rather than supporting long-term missionaries. The strategy and locations of short-term missions can sometimes become a 'marketing' point for individual churches.

North American congregations, mission committees, youth pastors, mission pastors, and individual Christians discovered that activities intended at least in part for the spiritual and educational benefit of themselves and their own membership could be funded in the name of "missions" — and could thus legitimately draw on the sacred rhetoric and funding apparatus pioneered by career missionaries. (Priest et al, 2006)

Most short-term mission teams are never actually involved in evangelism. Instead, most of their effort is geared towards development work and activities like building or painting schools and handing out food or medical supplies. 'Although globally aware, these young people seem unclear on what the Gospel is beyond just "doing good,"' writes Paul Borthwick in *Western Christians in Global Missions* (2012). He claims that modern missions are more recognised for low impact, quick projects and good deeds than for the proclamation of the Gospel to the lost.

Herein lies a fundamental crisis in missiology. The postmodern and pluralistic underpinnings of Western culture have dramatically influenced the mission efforts of the Western church. A 2015 Pew study revealed that 82% of Christians in the US believed in heaven, while only 67% believed in hell. In some mainline churches, only 56% said they believed in hell. Lacking any conviction about the eternal consequences of the Gospel, there is a lack of urgency in saving the lost, abroad or at home.

A long-term study conducted by Ver Beek (2006) surveyed 162 short-term missionaries who travelled to Honduras after the 1998 Hurricane Mitch. Ver Beek compared the impact of Christian short-term missions to the impact of local responses to the hurricane damage. One Christian agency sent 26 Canadian and five American teams to assist in the rebuilding of houses. The cost of sending each team was $30,000 and each team built one house. This totalled to a cost of $930,000 for building 31 houses. In stark contrast, local churches and local Christian organisations were able to construct houses for just $2,000 each. The North American sending Christian agency justified the additional cost arguing that the Western mission teams would have a greater spiritual impact on the Hondurans. However, Ver Beek concluded that 'the STM group had neither less nor greater impact than the Honduran Christian organizations despite the difference in amount spent.'

The local beneficiaries emphatically underlined this point. Ver Beek asked them if it would have been better if the Americans had sent money, which would have built 465 instead of merely 31 houses. The beneficiaries said that sending money would have met more needs and would have created jobs locally for those in desperate need of employment. Quite tellingly though, the beneficiaries doubted whether the Western Christians would ever choose to send money. Moreover, the Honduran interviewees did not feel that helping them was the main motivation or focus of the trips. Instead they 'believe such trips play important roles in helping North Americans learn and be changed' themselves. Interestingly, only 11% of the short-term team members reported significant changes in their prayer lives, volunteering or financial giving on their return. These trips had little or no tangible long-term impact on either the beneficiaries or the mission participants.

Missio Dei (mission of God) has become 'Missio Me' in the Western church, which exports this brand of mission enthusiastically and sends millions of short-term missionaries who are poorly equipped with a shallow understanding of theology and mission. 'Missio Me' is now a $4 billion industry.

CONTEXTUALISATION

Although God does not call all Christians to be overseas missionaries, He calls all of us to witness to the Gospel within our own context. In an effort to preach the Gospel more effectively, Christians have to bridge wisely the divides between Scripture and culture. The idea of contextualisation is not new. The apostle Paul alludes to this strategy in his first letter to the church at Corinth. 'To the Jews I became like a Jew, to win the Jews. To those under the law I became like one under the law (though I myself am not under the law), so as to win those under the law. To those not having the law I became like one not having the law (though I am not free from God's law but am under Christ's law), so as to win those not having the law. To the weak I became weak, to win the weak. I have become all things to all people so that by all possible means I might save some. I do all this for the sake of the gospel, that I may share in its blessings' (1 Corinthians 9:20-23).

Contextualisation is the process by which a church adapts to the prevailing culture. A church may use local styles of music, translate the Bible into local languages, or use indigenous symbols as a means of contextualising its worship services. The Church has been doing contextual theology since its inception. When preaching the Gospel to pagans in the Greek city of Athens, the cultural capital of the ancient world, Paul quotes the Cretan poet Epimenides when he says 'in him we live and move and have our being' (Acts 17:22-31). When Paul exhorts the Corinthians, 'Do not be misled: "Bad company corrupts good character,"' he cites the comic poet Menander (1 Corinthians 15:33). In his letter to Titus, he writes 'Even one of their own prophets has said, "Cretans are always liars, evil brutes, lazy gluttons,"' again quoting Epimenides (Titus 1:12).

Paul does not quote these pagan poets to support their teachings. He quotes them to build bridges with his hearers, gain credibility with them, earn the right to be heard and, in doing so, to defend and preach the Gospel. There are good reasons for contextualisation but also dangers and pitfalls.

Bevans (1992) calls contextualisation an 'imperative' and even 'inevitable' while Goheen (2001) states that contextualisation is the 'normal relation of the church to its culture.' The Church must be aware of the context within which she exists and must see varying sub-cultures not as threats but as opportunities to preach the Gospel. Christians must study developing ideologies and worldviews in different cultures and new models of communication to ensure that the message of Christ remains relevant.

The danger is that of capitulating completely to the context. When this happens, the church embraces culture to such an extent that she waters down and even rejects the doctrinal and moral absolutes of orthodox Christianity, simply because they are counter-cultural and go against the context. Recent examples of this include the legitimising of abortion, homosexuality and transgenderism in some mainline Western churches.

Less obvious, but particularly alarming, is the rise of the 'Insider Movement,' a mission strategy based on deception, which encourages converts from other religions to remain within their religious culture. The Insider Movement has become popular in the field of Muslim evangelism.

John Jay Travis, father of the Insider Movement, describes converts as staying 'legally and socially within the Islamic community,' even if 'in some contexts, this may mean active participation in Muslim religious life and practice' (Travis and Brown, 2009). Converts do not become 'Christian' but describe themselves as 'Followers of Isa' (the Muslim name for Jesus). The Muslim community in which these converts live would not recognise these converts as Christians but continue to identify them as Muslims. The converts would even consider themselves Muslims. Islamic doctrines and practices which are incompatible with the Bible are discouraged or 'cleverly reinterpreted if possible.' However, the Insider Movement gives no examples of Islamic practices they would completely reject. Rather, Insider converts worship in a mosque, read the Quran, observe all five pillars of Islam, including the Hajj (pilgrimage to Mecca, where non-Muslims are not allowed).

There are many similarities between the Insider Movement and the Seeker-Sensitive movement. Seeker-Sensitive churches aim to be appealing to potential converts or 'seekers.' Although there may be mature Christians in the congregation, services are almost completely designed for the unbeliever. The dress code is casual or contextualised to a particular age group or subculture (for example millennials, hipsters, goths, etc). Worship services consist of multimedia presentations, skits, dramatic performances, upbeat contemporary music by a live band, and short, practical, self-help sermons with very little exposition of the Bible. Secular media, music and film are often used. Difficult, challenging and controversial topics are avoided. Christian terms and symbols are removed or avoided. Christians sometimes do not call themselves Christians. Instead, they refer to themselves as Christ Followers or use similar labels. The Lord's Supper is hardly ever celebrated for fear of offending or confusing newcomers. Sometimes, attendees are not even invited to become members of the church or convert to Christianity — because they might be put off by 'commitment phobia.' Thus, congregants and seekers are not challenged on issues of sin, cultural compromise or any need to change their lifestyles. There is little discipleship and new Christians are encouraged to remain within their existing Western cultural structures as Insiders.

Dorothy Greco finds that 'many churches gradually, and perhaps unwittingly, transitioned from being appropriately sensitive to the needs of their congregants to becoming — if you'll permit some pop-psychologizing — co-dependent with them.' She explains what co-dependence looks like within a church. 'Avoiding sections of Scripture out of fear that certain power pockets will be offended. Believing that repeat attendance depends primarily upon the staff's seamless execution of Sunday morning — rather than the manifest presence of God. Eliminating doleful songs from the worship repertoire because they might contradict the thought line that "following Jesus is all gain."' What is the solution? 'Jesus understood that the irreducible gospel message — that we are all sinners in need of being saved — was, and always will be, offensive. No brilliant marketing campaign could ever repackage it,' she asserts.

Studies indicate that over-contextualisation, instead of drawing more unbelievers, actually drives them away. A five-year academic study entitled *Theology Matters: Comparing the Traits of Growing and declining Mainline Protestant Church Attendees and Clergy* (2016) by Haskell et al, demonstrates that churches that are theologically conservative or hold on to their orthodox interpretation of the Bible grow faster than those with a more liberal theology.

The leaders and congregants of growing churches are more theologically conservative and exhibit higher rates of Bible reading and prayer. Growing church congregants are more likely to agree that their congregation has a clear mission and purpose and to identify evangelism as that purpose.

WORSHIP

It has been said that when Christians celebrate the sacraments, they do so before a watching world, since the Christian community is part of society and the world. Thus Christian worship is the activity of the community "which see itself as living by grace, existing for the sake of others, welcoming strangers and concerned for the world — a community with a mission". (Forrester, et al 1993)

Van Leeuwen, (in Hestenes, 1999) says that 'those who grasp the little finger of liturgics [worship] will find that they have taken the whole hand of theology.' Worship is at the very heart of understanding God, the role of the Church in the world and the basics of the Christian faith. *Lex Orandi, Lex Credendi, Lex Vivendi.* As we worship, so we believe, so we live. Worship is the key to understanding the influence of Western culture on the church. Our understanding of the ultimate purpose of worship will influence how and why we worship.

Why is worship the primary and central activity of the church? What is the purpose of our worship? Is it to glorify God, or is it to attract consumers? Is worship a shop-window, an advertisement, a commercial, a means to an end, or is it an end in itself? 'To worship the Lord is — in the world's eyes — a waste of time. It is, indeed, a *royal* waste of time, but a waste nonetheless. By engaging in it, we don't accomplish anything useful in our society's terms,' argues theologian Marva J. Dawn. This runs entirely against the grain of a consumer society, where time is money and everything is a means to an end. What follows from the above understanding of worship is clear. 'Worship ought not to be construed in a utilitarian way. Its purpose is not to gain numbers nor for our churches to be seen as successful. Rather, the entire reason for our worship is that God deserves it.'

The first and foremost purpose of worship is to respond to God, says Bishop William Willimon (1993). 'In its most classic sense, worship has no other function than the joyful, ecstatic abandon that comes when we meet and are met by God. Any attempt to use worship to educate, manipulate, or titillate can be a serious perversion of worship.' This is precisely what has happened in many Western churches — and exported across continents. Instead of being God-focussed, worship is increasingly 'me-centred' and focussed on the emotional needs of the worshipper seeking to get 'high' on a 'worship experience.' The worship of God has been debased to a marketing tool to attract new customers into churches.

> Indeed, the so-called seeker-sensitive churches, well-meaning as they may be, put more emphasis upon what man will get out of a service of worship (unbeliever or believer) than upon what God will get out of it. To be sure, we are supposed to be seeker-sensitive when designing and executing worship, but according to Scripture, God (not man) is the Seeker toward whom we are to be sensitive in worship... In the New Covenant, as in the Old, Christians are called to worship God in the manner that He prescribes, and not according to the shifting desires and changing fads of the unbelieving culture. If we worship in God's Spirit and according to His truth, the object of our worship will inevitably be God Himself. In other words, our worship will be God-centred. Therefore, to make anything other than God the centre of our worship is, in a word, idolatry.
> — Jon D. Payne, *In the Splendor of Holiness* (2008)

In stark contrast, Pierson and Riddell, of The Prodigal Project, an 'emerging church' movement, actually see self-focus as one of the aims of worship. *The Prodigal Project* (2000) encourages prospective worshippers to 'start with who *you* are and work at growing a pattern of worship that is meaningful and authentic to you.'

Other churches see worship as a marketing tool to draw new believers or seekers. This turns the central purpose of worship upside down and with the focus on the seeker rather than on God, worship degenerates into entertainment — the service turns into a performance.

Robert E. Webber in *Ancient Future Worship* (2008) laments 'the crisis of worship' in the postmodern church and identifies the rise of 'entertainment or presentational worship.' Worship focused on the individual diminishes the role of the congregation. It becomes less participatory. Congregants become spectators who are there to be entertained. The criterion for evaluating worship is how it makes one feel and how much one enjoys it. Contrast this with the concept of worship as obedience, service and sacrifice as succinctly captured in the opening words of the Eucharistic Prayer in the Anglican *Book of Common Prayer* (1662): 'It is very meet, right, and our bounden duty, that we should at all times, and in all places, give thanks unto thee, O Lord, holy Father, almighty, everlasting God.'

Webber suggests that most evangelical churches have departed from the structure, style and content God intended for worship. He demonstrates how churches show:

a. A radical departure not only from the liturgies of the ancient church but from those of the Reformation as well

b. Confusion about order

c. Minimal use of the Bible

d. Passive congregations

e. A low view of the Lord's Supper

He suggests that these have had a significant effect not only on public worship but also on personal worship. He insists that in an effort to be evangelistic, 'relevant' to non-Christians, and 'attract a bigger audience,' the Church has embraced style at the expense of tradition. He believes that, ironically, this has made the modern Church less relevant and effective in evangelism and that she has in essence become secular. 'Thus worship, which stands at the very centre of our Christian experience, having been secularised, is unable to feed, nourish, enhance, challenge, inspire and shape the collective and individual life of our congregations in the way it should. Consequently, the whole evangelical movement suffers.'

John Goldingay (2009) commenting on Christian symbols and tradition, states that worship needs both to 'reflect the culture outside church and to be distinguished from it.' He suggests that traditional liturgical worship focuses more on the second, while evangelical worship, in order to be culturally relevant and attractive to outsiders, focuses on the first. The worship of the early Church included 'the Old and New Testament practices of liturgy, baptism, symbolic feasts that became the Eucharist, and certain of the feast days.'

Webber agrees that the use of traditions and symbols serves as a way of remembering God's provision and 'saving deeds' not only in our lives but also in the history of the world. The church does this through 'historical recitation' in the form of songs, preaching and creeds as well as through 'dramatic re-enactment' in baptism, Bible reading and Holy Communion.

How, then, does the church strike a balance between content and context? The content of worship should not be isolated from the context of worship. Context is what makes the content relevant. Content-laden worship runs the risk of becoming exclusive only to those who understand it. Instead, churches should guide Christians through the content in a way that enables them to understand it. At the same time, context should not be the sole determiner of content. Rather, content should challenge the context and seek to transform it.

Marva Dawn writes, '...I am intensely troubled that so many church leaders seem to want never to demand anything of worshippers. Of course, I am not advocating the opposite extreme of making everything too hard for the people to participate. It is important, however, in between those two extremes, that congregations *do all they can to counteract the present idea* that we must do all we can to make worship easy for those who come so that they'll come back again.'

From age to age, churches have adapted their musical styles to reflect the tastes of the prevailing culture. As these changes take place, there have always been some who lament these modifications of style. Sometimes reservations about modern trends are a reaction to a change in style rather than a reaction to a change in the content of worship itself. Nevertheless, style and substance, form and content, are often intertwined. When change in style dilutes or distorts the very content of worship, it is time for the church to sit up and take notice.

The study by Haskell et al also found that services of growing churches featured contemporary music, with drums and guitars. This indicates that although a church can be relevant in some aspects to the culture in which it exists, if it does not compromise the core theological beliefs as laid down in the Bible it will thrive. Churches that succumb to the prevailing humanist, postmodern, liberal elements of the culture are in danger of decline.

Paradoxically, this decline may have to do with a thirst for truth in a postmodern era. A tsunami of information and misinformation washes up on our digital shores every single minute of the day. People simply no longer know who or what to trust. Churches are compromising their historic beliefs and their historic focus on Scripture, tradition, reason and experience of growing in Christ-likeness through our daily walk with Him. The aim is apparently to be cool, trendy, relevant and to seek experience in the sense of an 'emotional high.' This may 'fool some of the people some of the time' but they will soon be relegated to the trashcan of history as insubstantial, unreliable and uncertain in their convictions, mission and values. They remain unattractive to those who yearn for unambiguous truth.

5
CHRISTIANITY IN A POST-TRUTH AND POSTMODERN WORLD

POST-TRUTH — an adjective defined as 'relating to or denoting circumstances in which objective facts are less influential in shaping public opinion than appeals to emotion and personal belief.' (Oxford Dictionaries Word of the Year, 2016)

Truthiness [post-truth] is tearing apart our country . . . I don't know whether it's a new thing, but it's certainly a current thing, in that it doesn't seem to matter what facts are. It used to be, everyone was entitled to their own opinion, but not their own facts. But that's not the case anymore. Facts matter not at all. Perception is everything. It's certainty. — Stephen Colbert (2006)

INTRODUCTION

What is truth? Does truth matter? Is absolute truth obsolete in the postmodern world? Is it imperative for Christians speak the truth, the whole truth and nothing but the truth? How do Christians speak truth to power? Aroon Purie, editor-in-chief of *India Today* would tell his reporters, 'Somewhere someone is out to hide the truth. Find that. That is news. All the rest is merely advertisement.'

Journalists, philosophers and academics in the postmodern West would ridicule Purie's definition of news and his understanding of truth. There has been a fundamental shift in how we understand truth. We are currently living in what is being termed the 'post-truth' era. Truth is no longer regarded as the essential value on which Western society is built. Post-truth is now an accepted ideology and methodology that has infiltrated society at all levels. It is now widely considered permissible, if not acceptable, to lie. Lying, deception and spin doctoring have even come to be regarded as virtues and an industry.

WHAT IS TRUTH?

Truth is a complicated concept to define. It has many aspects and its definition has been debated for millennia. Each culture, religion, ideology and language seems to have its own understanding of truth. Postmodern philosophers claim that there can be no absolute truth. The prestigious *Stanford Encyclopaedia of Philosophy* states that truth is relative and that 'truth and falsity, right and wrong, standards of reasoning, and procedures of justification are products of differing conventions and frameworks of assessment and that their authority is confined to the context giving rise to them.' By contrast, philosophers of a more traditional persuasion insist that there are absolute truths that are irrefutable.

'What is truth?' (John 18:38) It is hard to imagine a more profound question with more momentous consequences. The most clearly articulated theory of truth among the Greek philosophers is by Aristotle

(384-322 BC). 'To say that that which is, is not, or that which is not is, is a falsehood; and to say that that which is, is, and that which is not is not, is true.' In modern philosophical language, we would paraphrase Aristotle thus: The truth of a sentence consists in its agreement with reality.

Truth in the Old Testament is not defined philosophically, but relationally. Its root idea is faithfulness — firmness, steadfastness, trustworthiness, reliability, sureness. On the one hand, truth refers to the faithfulness of God. On the other hand, truth refers to human beings demonstrating faithfulness by living and speaking the truth.

Most people unconsciously subscribe to the correspondence theory of truth, championed by Plato and Aristotle. Here, 'truth is correspondence with the facts' or 'truth is agreement with reality.' Truth is the agreement between a statement of fact and an actual state of affairs. The statement 'dogs bark' is true because of the fact that dogs bark. A statement is true if there exists a fact corresponding to it. We will define truth as words corresponding to actual, objective reality or facts.

The Post-Truth Era

This is not the first time that a society based on the Judeo-Christian worldview has become a post-truth society. Augustine of Hippo wrote in the fourth century:

> Why, then, does truth generate hatred, and why does thy servant who preaches the truth come to be an enemy to them who also love the happy life, which is nothing else than joy in the truth — unless it be that truth is loved in such a way that those who love something else besides her wish that to be the truth which they do love.... Therefore, they hate the truth for the sake of whatever it is that they love in place of the truth. They love truth when she shines on them; and hate her when she rebukes them.

There are some major contributors to our current ideology of post-truth.

Philosophical Contributors

The ancient Greek philosophy of Scepticism is one of the earliest attempts at deconstructing the notion of truth. On the one hand, the sceptics believed that life should be devoted to genuine inquiry. They did not deny that knowledge could be found. On the other hand, the sceptics would suspend judgement and not affirm anything as long as knowledge of something had not been attained. This resulted in a paradox: one could live life without believing anything. But the claim that 'nothing can be known' is itself a claim to know something! Scepticism is thus a self-refuting philosophy.

A contemporary of Scepticism was Sophism, founded by the Greek philosopher Protagoras who taught that truth is subjective and relative. Sophism is often credited with being the father of moral relativism. Sophists specialised in using clever rhetoric to win arguments, regardless of truth. They believed that whatever you can make people believe through strong arguments, regardless of reality, is truth. Protagoras taught that knowledge and truth were at best only opinion since a human being could obtain only partial knowledge based on partial experience. He is famously quoted as saying, 'What is true for you is true for you, and what is true for me is true for me. Truth is totally subjective.'

Historians of ideas divide Western culture into three periods: the pre-modern, the modern and the postmodern. The period of Christendom before the Renaissance and Reformation is considered pre-modern. Pre-modern society was characterised by belief in the supernatural and an acceptance of the authority of the church and religion. The Wars of Religion (1618-1648) in Europe put an end to the pre-modern era. Then came the Enlightenment, giving rise to modernism with a philosophical shift from faith to fact, from acceptance to questioning of all authority of the church and the Bible. The Enlightenment believed in reason alone as the highest authority. It believed that progress was inevitable, science was invincible and democracy was desirable. It upheld truth as absolute, objective and universal, believing that it was possible to discover the truth through rational inquiry and scientific investigation. The Enlightenment moved from faith to fact, from belief to reason.

Some of the more radical philosophers of the Enlightenment (1650-1800) revived the seeds sown by the philosophies of Scepticism and Sophism and questioned the existence of God and the truth of Scripture. David Hume (1711-1776), Immanuel Kant (1724-1804), and Karl Marx (1818-1883) began to question not just God and morality but the very nature of reality. For them, truth and reality were open to interpretation and were not be trusted.

The most radical of the Enlightenment philosophers who sought to debunk the very notion of truth was the German atheist Friedrich Nietzsche with his dictum 'truth is fiction.'

The majority of Enlightenment philosophers who had rejected a belief in God, still retained belief in Christian moral principles. This seems like a contradiction in terms, but because modernism believed in truth, it consequently accepted universal norms for truth and falsehood, good and evil, right and wrong. Nietzsche's writings were a great influence on Michel Foucault (1924-1984), a leading French philosopher who began to question the very idea of truth and thus opened the flood gates of a new movement called postmodernism. By the late 19th century, Nietzsche had begun to question how Enlightenment philosophers could continue to uphold Christian morality if they no longer believed in God. 'There are no moral facts whatever. Moral judgement has this in common with religious judgement — that it believes in realities which do not exist,' wrote Nietzsche. If, as Nietzche famously said, 'God is dead,' there is no reason why Christian morality should remain alive.

As Foucault said in an interview: 'I think that, instead of trying to find out what truth, as opposed to error, is, it might be more interesting to take up the program posed by Nietzsche: how is it that, in our societies, "the truth" has been given this value, thus placing us absolutely under its thrall.'

Foucault and his contemporaries ushered in the new age of postmodernism. If pre-modernism was based on faith, and modernism on fact, postmodernism is based on feeling. Nike's slogan 'Just do it' captures postmodern morality in a nutshell. If you think it is right just do it. If it feels good it must be right. Different strokes for different folks. Don't think too much about it. Go with your gut. It just feels right. It just feels good. I am not hurting anyone.

There are no absolutes in postmodern thinking. There is no absolute truth. The only absolute is the absence of absolutes. Hence, there are no foundational norms for morality. Truth is relative. The postmodern American philosopher Richard Rorty unapologetically proclaims, 'There is no truth. We should give up the search for truth and be content with interpretations.' Hence, morality is a matter of preference or perspective. It all depends on how you see it.

CHARACTERISTICS AND CONSEQUENCES OF A POST-TRUTH SOCIETY

And what happens when you give up your conviction that truth can be discovered, and instead promote the idea that all ways of looking at the world, and interpreting the world, and feeling the world, have validity? You disorientate public discussion. You slay your own cultural authority. You create a situation where people doubt you, often with good reason, and go looking for other sources of information. You create the space for other claims of truth, some of them good and exciting, some of them mad and fake — "Fake News," "Post-truth" and All the Rest. (Stuttaford, 2016)

Lies are excused or accepted
'I think sometimes we can disagree with the facts.' — Sean Spicer, Press Secretary to US President Donald Trump. *The Guardian* (2017)

Instead of people questioning facts or challenging those who try to pass falsities as facts they are ignored, excused or even embraced. Lying is no longer called lying. We speak of 'alternative facts,' people are 'economical with the truth,' facts are 'sweetened,' or 'improved,' and realities are 'redefined.' Instead of calling people liars, we say they 'may have misspoken,' or 'misrepresented the truth' or, at best, 'exercised poor judgment.'

Lying is intentional and encouraged

The aim of lying is to persuade someone that something that is not real is real, mostly for purpose of gaining an advantage. Lying and deception have been part of military strategy for centuries. Sun Tzu said, 'All war is deception' (*The Art of War*, 5th century BC). The invasion of Normandy on D-Day during the Second World War was preceded by a huge and elaborate deception plan aimed at misleading the Nazi forces. During the Cold War, deception strategies became almost scientific in their use and deployment. Psychological and information operations and propaganda became part of societal fabric and were elevated to new heights. Management of facts, truth, and perception was not just focused on enemy forces, but also communicated to home populations. Governments used propaganda and false facts in almost all aspects of society, from schools, pop-culture and media, to indoctrinate populations in favour of or in opposition to certain ideologies, to justify their actions and to gain loyal, almost unquestioning, support.

This strategy was picked up by large business corporations. Harvard Business School teaches 'strategic misrepresentation,' which is a term for the apparently laudable 'tactic of hiding facts, bluffing, or lying during a business negotiation.' (Peters, 2017) With gigantic strides in digital technology and social media, propaganda and falsities are mass-produced and mass consumed. Deception is seen as a means to an end, and the ability to bend truth and manage the narrative, never mind the facts, is presented as a virtue.

Choosing to believe falsehoods

One of the defining characteristics of a post-truth society is the choices people make when evaluating information. Truth, if it exists, is seen as secondary to emotion and ideological positions. People make choices based on how it makes them feel and whether it confirms or contradicts their already established points of view or dogmatism.

Internet search engines like Google reinforce such behaviour observes Siva Vaidhyanathan in his book *The Googlization of Everything (and Why We Should Worry)*. 'Overwhelmingly, we now allow Google to determine what is important, relevant, and true on the Web and in the world.' But 'Google causes damage mostly by crowding out other alternatives,' he writes. How does this work? Every time you post a message to your Facebook wall or Google the name of your favourite celebrity you leave a digital trail. These tiny trails are aggregated to create a profile of your personality. Google, Yahoo, Facebook and other Internet giants personalize this information to feed you data they think you want to know and they think you ought to know. They supply you only with search results that confirm your existing beliefs and prejudices. They filter out information that will challenge what you like or believe. They surround you with like-minded people who will tell you what you want to hear. The aim is to get you to click more, like more, and buy more.

Moreover, search engines and social media have become an echo chamber in which the person's own views are reinforced by like-minded people and their presuppositions are rarely challenged. Carole Cadwalladr demonstrates how Google's search algorithms reflect virtually nothing but the popularity of the most-responded to sites for the search enquiry. There is no check on whether any of the information is actually true or reliable. Cadwalladr was particularly alarmed when she typed in 'Are Jews...' and before she could finish, Google's search engines had provided the most likely responses, one of which was 'Are Jews evil?' Curious, she hit that entry, and was taken to the authoritative Google page of the 10 most common and popular answers, 9 of 10 of which said, in effect, 'Yes, definitely, Jews are evil.'

Psychologically, when people are presented with information that confirms what they already believe to be true, bursts of pleasure are triggered in their brains. Conversely, when you present people with information that challenges what they believe, they get cranky. The Internet companies know this. They build filters to surround us with information that is agreeable to us and not with information that's uncomfortable, Eli Pariser points out in his book *The Filter Bubble: What the Internet Is Hiding from You* (2011).

People do not challenge lies or liars

Truth is the new hate speech. — Rush Limbaugh (2012)

People are too scared to challenge lies, because they themselves do not know what to believe or are afraid to offend people with the truth. In a post-truth age people are encouraged to believe anything or even do anything without fear of the consequences. People find their identity in dogmatically held personal beliefs and worldviews, which often have no basis in facts and realities. Hence, to question a person's belief or behaviour, even if it does not stand up to an empirical or philosophical analysis, is to question their very identity or existence. Many Western countries have begun to legislate against such truth speech, deeming it to be highly offensive and tantamount to hate crime or hate speech.

The most recent example of this is transgenderism, where someone who is born with the biological body parts of one gender chooses to identify themselves as the other gender. To refer to this choice as questionable or wrong, even though it flies in the face of the most basic scientific and empirical facts, is now illegal in many countries.

The prophet Jeremiah paints a vivid picture of a society where even prophets are afraid to speak truth to power. The political lie dominating the official narrative during the time of Jeremiah was that Babylon would not attack Israel and that there would be peace rather than hostility. The false prophets and the priests pacified the people with the phony prophecy of '"Peace, peace," when there is no peace,' cries Jeremiah (Jeremiah 6:13-14; 8:11).

Injustice thrives

In a post-truth age, unrighteousness and injustice thrive. If there is no truth and there is no right or wrong, gross injustices are ignored, excused or not believed. Walter Brueggemann points out that the ninth commandment (Exodus 20:16) links 'false witness' with 'neighbour' because 'viable community ... depends upon accurate, reliable utterance.' Kerstin Tuschik emphatically underlines this meltdown of community as a consequence of a post-truth ideology. 'When facts stop mattering, which unfortunately has become the norm in our so-called post-truth and post-fact culture, the core structure of society breaks down,' she states.

Moreover, the setting for the ninth commandment is the judicial context, which depends on truth-telling by reliable witnesses who must offer honest testimony.

Lying becomes a habit

Dan Ariely, sociologist and author of *Deception*, released a study in 2015 which stated:

> Dishonesty is an integral part of our social world, influencing domains ranging from finance and politics to personal relationships. Anecdotally digressions from a moral code are often described as a series of small breaches that grow over time. Here we provide empirical evidence for a gradual escalation of self-serving dishonesty and reveal a neural mechanism supporting it. Behaviourally we show that the extent to which participants engage in self-serving dishonesty increases with repetition. The findings uncover a biological mechanism that supports a "slippery slope;" what begins as a small act of dishonesty can escalate into larger transgressions. (Ariely, Garret, Lazzaro, & Sharot, 2016)

The more we lie, the more we become used to lying and the easier lying gets. Big lies exist because of small lies. Small lies escalate into big lies.

Other studies suggest that lying is actually good. *Forbes* magazine reported a study suggesting that adolescents who are most popular with their peers were the ones that were the best at being deceptive. (Rose, 2005). A University of Pennsylvania study introduced the term 'benevolent deception' suggesting that deception and lying are, in some cases, for the greater good. (Schweitzer & Levine, 2014). The study concluded that 'little white lies' are not only permissible but should be promoted and considered moral. 'Lying Children Will Grow Up to be Successful Citizens,' was the headline of a *Telegraph* article reporting a study which states that children as young as two should be encouraged to lie because it teaches and promotes creativity. (Alleyne, 2010)

The consequences of such endemic deception are catastrophic. Ralph Keyes in his book *The Post-truth Era: Dishonesty and Deception in Contemporary Life* underlines the end-result of such a culture.

> The more we lie the more we become used to it. This is post-truth. In the post-truth era, borders blur between truth and lies, honesty and dishonesty, fiction and nonfiction. Deceiving others becomes a challenge, a game, and ultimately a habit.

The Church is not immune to post-truth
Post-truth and deception are not confined to secular society. The church has been influenced by the post-truth phenomenon and has been at times complicit in its spread.

A 2016 article in *Christianity Today* identifies the five big lies pastors tell — how big their church is, how healthy the church is, how spiritually and emotionally strong they are, how strong and stable their marriage and family are, and how sure they are about their church's direction. Likewise, some Christian leaders and missionaries report 'fake news' concerning their evangelistic successes, for example, in newsletters hugely exaggerating the number of converts they have made and the success of their ministries. This seems to happen particularly when the missionaries depend on the readers of those newsletters for their financial support.

Another area of lying is plagiarism — which is also stealing. To use someone else's sermons or writings without acknowledging or giving credit to the original preacher or author is deception. Over the last few years, a number of high-profile Christian leaders have been accused of plagiarism in the pulpit and in their books. Seattle megachurch pastor Mark Driscoll was accused in 2014 of plagiarism by Tyndale House Publishers and InterVarsity Press. Driscoll apologised after the plagiarism was exposed. Around the same time, Oklahoma City based megachurch pastor Craig Groeschel was accused of plagiarizing the work of writer and comedian Danny Murphy in a book titled *Love, Sex, and Happily Ever After,* printed by Multnomah Books. In 2013, Episcopal priest John E. McGinn from Massachusetts was accused of plagiarizing sermons from Sermons.com and suspended by his diocese. Even Richard Land, former president of the Southern Baptist Convention's Ethics and Religious Liberty Commission, came under fire in 2012 after being accused of plagiarism in his radio broadcasts.

The Western Church has in fact been prone to deceptive practices for many centuries. In the late Middle Ages, Roman Catholics developed a doctrine known as 'mental reservation.' This permitted a person to speak only part of a truthful answer, 'reserving' the rest of the sentence in their mind for God alone. In some cases, the speaker mentally adds some qualification to the words which they utter, and the words together with the mental qualification constitutes the whole truth. There had to be special circumstances to justify the use of mental reservation, for example, the threat of persecution as in 16th and 17th century England. This became such a major issue that whole treatises were written on it and the practice was finally banned by Pope Innocent XI in 1679. It has now re-emerged in the various sexual abuse scandals afflicting the Catholic Church (See, for example, the Irish government's 2009 Murphy Report into sexual abuse in the Archdiocese of Dublin).

Closely linked to this is the concept of 'equivocation' which has at times been accepted by Christians from a variety of denominations, especially Anglicans. This is a kind of wordplay where, by using words with double meanings, people can successfully deceive the listener or reader without blatantly lying.

The extreme contextualisation practised by some modern Western missionaries — and which they teach to converts — involves a great deal of mental reservation and equivocation, if not outright lying. For example, the Christian missionary, when asked by a Muslim about their religion, will not admit to being a Christian but will reply, 'I am a true Muslim.' This is classic equivocation, in which the speaker uses the word 'Muslim' to mean in their own mind 'someone submitted to God' (as a devout Christian should be) knowing full well that the hearer will understand the word to mean a follower of Islam.

Living in a post-truth era, Christians often seem to believe that they can practise mental reservation, equivocation, lying and plagiarism and get away with it. The justification is based on the principle of 'protection of the institution as paramount, sacrifice of the individual a regrettable necessity.' It is alarmingly close to the classical Islamic concept of *taqiyya* which permits lying in some specific circumstances. Many Islamic scholars list these circumstances as defending Islam and its good name, a man speaking to his wife, or patching up a quarrel between two people. Unfortunately, some Christians broaden this to lie for their own self-interest or their personal objectives.

HOW SHOULD THE CHURCH ACT IN A POST-TRUTH CULTURE?

Douglas Groothuis, in his book *Truth Decay*, writes, 'Without a thorough and deeply rooted understanding of the biblical view of truth, the Christian response to postmodernism will be muted by the surrounding culture or will make illicit compromises with the truth-impoverished spirit of the age.'

As we have already seen, truth in the Old Testament is not defined philosophically, but relationally. In Genesis 42:16, Joseph not only speaks of truth but also makes explicit the notion of testing and verifying the truth: 'Send one of your number to get your brother; the rest of you will be kept in prison, so that your words may be tested to see if you are telling the truth. If you are not, then as surely as Pharaoh lives, you are spies!' In the law-book of Deuteronomy 'truth' is understood in a forensic or legal sense — that which is obtained by rigorous and through investigation. E.g. '...then you must inquire, probe and investigate it thoroughly. And if it is true and it has been proved that this detestable thing has been done among you' (Deuteronomy 13:14). Above all, God himself is 'truth' in two senses. He alone is the 'true' God. 'But the Lord is the true God; he is the living God, the eternal King' (Jeremiah 10:10). And He is 'true' in the sense of being faithful. 'The

Lord God, pitiful and merciful, longsuffering and very compassionate, and true,' is how the Greek version of the Old Testament renders it. 'And the Lord passed by before him, and proclaimed, The Lord, The Lord God, merciful and gracious, longsuffering, and abundant in goodness and truth' (Exodus 34:6 KJV).

The prophet Jeremiah offers a four-point lie-detector test to uncover the false prophets. The false prophets are those whom God has not called to speak for Him. 'I have not sent them or appointed them or spoken to them' (Jeremiah 14:14). First, they are in ministry for the money. 'From the least to the greatest, all are greedy for gain; prophets and priests alike, all practice deceit' (Jeremiah 6:13). They are prophets for profits. Second, they have low moral standards — they are drunkards, adulterers, and idolaters (Jeremiah 13:13).Third, their theology is fanciful. It is the figment of their imagination. It is not rooted in God's revelation. It panders to the politically correct demands of the day. 'They speak visions from their own minds, not from the mouth of the Lord' (Jeremiah 23:16). Fourth, their prophecies will be proved false.

John tells us in his Gospel that Jesus is 'full of grace and truth' (John 1:14, 17) and the 'way, the truth and the life' (John 14:6). He records that Jesus tells Pilate that He has come 'to testify to the truth' and that everyone who 'belongs to the truth' listens to His voice (John 18:37). 'Then you will know the truth, and the truth will set you free,' He tells His disciples (John 8:32). He will send the 'Spirit of truth who will testify on my behalf' (John 15:26). And when the 'But when he, the Spirit of truth, comes, he will guide you into all the truth' (John 16:13).

There are three main aspects to our response to the post-truth era.

We Must be Beyond Reproach
Our own words and actions must be beyond reproach. We cannot let our minds, mouths or actions succumb to believing, telling or spreading lies. This could be difficult as we may already be influenced by the culture in which we live. With so many lies, it would be unusual not to have been somehow influenced in some way. The more we submit to

the web of deceit, the more we too, can end up believing that lying is permissible and even good at times.

We may avoid stating truths in case they cause offence. The more we avoid the truth the more we begin to believe the lies that surround us. The more the culture around us corrodes the truth the more we have to stand firm. Our first action should be repenting and seeking forgiveness for any lies or deception we have committed. Through personal commitment to the truth and with the help of the Holy Spirit, we are able to move towards a state of righteousness and truthfulness.

We Must Know what is True and False
We must be conscious of deceptions and falsehoods that try and steer us from the truth. At times, we may have even consciously chosen not to believe reality or facts because they challenged our established point of view, lifestyle or made us uncomfortable. We believed what we wanted to believe.

We must test facts and use common sense. In our use of social media, we must be careful not to repost reports without first verifying them. The more false reports we post, the less the authority of our witness in the world. We should pray and ask the Lord to reveal areas in our lives where we ourselves have been deceived. We may also seek the Holy Spirit's gift of discernment and wisdom to help us discover the truth supernaturally.

We Must Stand Up For Truth
The third response is to stand for truth and against lies and falseness in the world. All human societies have a propensity towards maintaining the status quo of settled power arrangements. Such power structures seek to silence dissent and truth-telling. They seek to manage and manipulate public discourse. They seek to dumb down our critical faculties. They drip-feed us on a diet of compulsive consumerism. They create a culture of fear. The temptation is for Christians to retreat into our corner and hope that we will not be disturbed.

But this should not dissuade Christians and the Church from standing up for justice, righteousness and ultimately the truth.

Warren Wiersbe famously said, 'Truth without love is brutality, and love without truth is hypocrisy.' As Christians, we are called to balance love and truth. If we speak the truth without love, we can come across as angry, bigoted, judgmental, harsh and unforgiving. However, if we just love without speaking truth, we are doing a disservice to those we love and to society.

What is certain is that we must stand for truth. The concept of post-truth is not new to humankind. Isaiah 59:14-15 says:

> So justice is driven back,
> and righteousness stands at a distance;
> truth has stumbled in the streets,
> honesty cannot enter.
> Truth is nowhere to be found,
> and whoever shuns evil becomes a prey.
> The Lord looked and was displeased
> that there was no justice.

6
CHILDREN, FAMILY AND EDUCATION

We tried to defend the unborn child, the dignity of the family, but it was a holding action. We are awash in evil and the battle is still to be waged. We are right now in the most discouraging period of that long conflict. Humanly speaking, we can say we have lost all those battles. — James Dobson, founder of *Focus of the Family*, at his retirement speech (2009)

... whether Dobson and his cohorts give up now or not, his assessment about their lack of success is nevertheless accurate. The culture war is all but over, and far-right evangelicals have precious little to show for their efforts. After about three decades of fighting, the culture warriors are hard pressed to point to *any* progress at all. — Steve Benen, columnist for *Washington Monthly* (2009)

Benen strikes a bleak note. Writing in the wake of Dobson's defeatist declaration, he depressingly goes on to point out that the anti-gay movement is all but vanquished in the US, with four states permitting gay marriage, abortion legalised, the majority of Americans being pro-choice, and school prayer no longer 'even on the political world's radar.' As if that were not gloomy enough, 'Pornography is not only a multi-billion industry; it's more accessible than ever.'

Today, same-sex marriage is legal in all fifty states in America, with over 63% of the population in favour of same-sex marriages in 2016. In 2001, Forbes estimated that the US pornography industry was worth $4 billion annually. By 2015, according to NBC, the US was contributing $10-12 billion annually to the global pornography industry.

The darkness deepens and gloom turns to doom, with the emergence of a number of alarming trends that threaten the traditional value-systems of children, families and education.

STATE INTERFERENCE IN PARENTING

In 2014, the Scottish National Party (SNP) announced the *Named Person Scheme*, seeking to appoint a 'Named Person' for every child in Scotland. The named person would be a state official tasked with looking after a child's 'wellbeing,' that is, their 'happiness.' This state guardian would be put in place regardless of whether or not children or parents wished to have one and regardless of whether there was any specific need for state intervention. The named person would have the power to check if children got a say in how their room was decorated and what they watched on TV and would be allowed to speak to a child, even about very personal issues, and provide the child with information or advice — all without requiring parental consent.

Five UK Supreme Court judges unanimously struck down the central provisions of the scheme in 2016, requiring the SNP to amend it. In June 2017, the Scottish Government released a watered-down version of the original plan, which makes clear that any advice offered by a named person is optional. This form of government intrusion into families is not restricted to Scotland.

In 2016, a Christian family in England engaged in a dispute with local authorities who were encouraging a 14-year-old girl to change her name to a boy's name because she believes she is transgender. The parents felt she was too young to make a choice about her gender and the school, social services and local government should not be involved in the matter. The mother said the child could make a choice about her own gender when she becomes an adult at the age of 18. Speaking anonymously, the parents told the media:

> The rights of parents in the UK are being eroded, especially those who have traditional Christian values. It is leaving parents to feel fearful, vulnerable and intimidated. We were told by the psychiatrist that Child and Adolescent Mental Health Services said that if the name change does not happen then she would be a high suicide risk. (Morley, 2016)

In June 2017, the state of Ontario, Canada, passed the *Supporting Children, Youth and Families Act*, known as Bill 89. The law mandates that child welfare agencies and family judges take into consideration 'race, ancestry, place of origin, colour, ethnic origin, citizenship, family diversity, disability, creed, sex, sexual orientation, gender identity and gender expression' when deciding whether or not a child should remain with their parents or foster families.

So if parents discriminate against their children on the basis of gender identity or sexual orientation, the state can remove the children from the parents, says Minister of Child and Family Services Michael Couteau. He describes this discrimination as 'a form of abuse when a child identifies as one way and a caregiver [parent] is saying "No, you need to do this differently" ... a child can be removed from that environment and placed into protection where the abuse stops.'

In addition, the Canadian government is able to intervene if there is 'a risk that that the child is likely to suffer emotional harm ... and that the child's parent or the person having charge of the child does not provide services or treatment' for, among other things, sexual orientation and gender identity. In other words, if a child displays gender dysphoria, and the parents do not take the child for hormone treatment or surgery to facilitate gender transition, the government could remove the children and charge the parents with abuse.

Moreover, the new legislation requires the parents to 'direct the child or young person's education and upbringing, in accordance with the child's or young person's creed, community identity and cultural identity.' This reverses legislation thus far in force, which states that 'the parent of a child in care retains any right...to direct the child's education and religious upbringing.' Parents suspected of enforcing a religious belief on their children could have their children removed.

In April 2016, two children in Ontario, aged three and five, were removed from their Christian foster parents, because the parents refused to say that the mythical Easter Bunny is real. The social workers told the parents that belief in the Easter Bunny was an important part of Canadian culture. Confused, the parents asked if the social worker believed in the existence of the Easter Bunny herself. The social worker admitted that it was a mythical creature, but insisted that if the parents did not tell the children that it was real, she would remove the children.

In court, parents Derek and Frances Baars said that they considered 'all lying to be morally wrong' because of their Christian beliefs. When applying to be foster parents, the Baars had informed Child Welfare Services that they would not celebrate Halloween or affirm belief in the Easter Bunny or Santa Claus.

CHRISTIANITY IS DANGEROUS TO CHILDREN

In 2011, a Pentecostal Christian couple lost their right to foster children after a British High Court ruled that laws protecting homosexuals from discrimination 'should take precedence' over the right not to be discriminated against on religious grounds. Eunice and Owen Johns had told a social worker that they could not tell a child a 'homosexual lifestyle' was acceptable.

The Christian Legal Centre (CLC), who provided legal aid to Mr and Mrs Johns, warned that 'fostering by Christians is now in doubt.' According to the CLC, the judgement effectively condemned, 'Biblical Christian beliefs' as 'inimical' to children, and implicitly upheld an Equality and Human Rights Commission (ECHC) submission that children risk being 'infected' by Christian moral beliefs. The judgment 'sends out the clear message that orthodox Christian ethical beliefs are potentially harmful to children and that Christian parents with mainstream Christian views are not suitable to be considered as potential foster parents,' the CLC said.

American psychologist Phil Zuckerman describes the time he took his older daughter to visit a Catholic mission in California as part of a school assignment. His daughter ran out of the chapel crying after seeing crucifixes with the image of Jesus dying on the cross. Zuckerman concludes that the fundamental doctrines of Christianity that we are all sinners and that 'God killed his own child to make up for our wickedness' are some of the 'abusive aspects of Christian theology.'

Oxford biologist and militant atheist Richard Dawkins claims that teaching children religion as fact constitutes child abuse. 'What a child should never be taught is that you are a Catholic or Muslim child, therefore that is what you believe. That's child abuse,' he said, speaking at the Chipping Norton Literary Festival.

Western governments are systematically stripping parents of their fundamental rights to impart moral and religious teaching to their children. Nowhere is this more pernicious than within the school system.

SCHOOLS AND EDUCATION

In June 2017, Scotland's largest teachers union announced that it had resolved to 'affiliate to the Time for Inclusive Education (TIE) campaign,' which aims at introducing LGBT education to all schools, including faith schools in Scotland. In February 2017, 67 members of the Scottish Parliament had signed TIE's campaign pledge, committing their support to the group's strategic proposals for LGBT inclusive education. Thus, the

Scottish Parliament became the first government in Europe to indicate majority support for the mandatory teaching of LGBT issues in schools.

The TIE campaign includes compulsory teaching on:

- Homophobia, biphobia, and transphobia
- Same-sex relationships
- The history of the gay rights movement and Stonewall
- Sexualities and sexual orientation
- Transsexualism and gender identity
- Pro-LGBT sexual health education

Parents would not be able to exclude their children from attending such education, regardless of their religious beliefs. In fact, faith schools were specifically singled out as requiring this type of education the most. Rev David Robertson of the Free Church of Scotland believes the TIE campaign is a dilution of the rights of Christian parents and the real objective is to indoctrinate school pupils with one particular perspective on moral and sexual ethics, a perspective that is contrary to Christianity.

In England, a Jewish school has been threatened with closure by the Office of Standards in Education, Children's Services and Skills (Ofsted), the education authority in England. This is because the ultra-Orthodox school, teaching girls aged three to eight, is refusing to educate pupils about homosexuality and transgenderism. Vishnitz Girls School is one of seven faith schools that failed an Ofsted inspection in the space of a few weeks in 2017. Although faith schools in the UK are not required to follow the national curriculum laid out for state schools, it is mandatory for them to follow standards for sex education issued by both the Department for Education and Ofsted. 'Ofsted has revealed its true agenda. It doesn't matter how good your school is in all other respects — simply refusing to teach very young children about gender reassignment will lead to your closure,' commented educator Gill Robbins on the blog of *Christians in Education*.

Authorities in Europe have also attempted to clamp down on home schooling. Armed German police stormed a house in Darmstadt in

August 2013, because the family living in the house were home schooling their four children. The children, between seven and fourteen years old, were forcibly removed from their parents, Dirk and Petra Wunderlich, and taken into state custody at an unknown location. The court transferred formal legal custody of the Wunderlich children to the state, despite there being no allegations of abuse or neglect against the parents, because their Christian parents wanted to raise them according to their own values. The authorities had already confiscated the children's passports to prevent the family from moving to neighbouring countries where home schooling is legal. Home schooling has been illegal in Germany since Hitler banned it in 1938.

In 2008, Uwe and Hannelore Romeike, two German evangelicals, requested political asylum in the US because they faced persecution in Germany for home schooling their six children. This was granted to them in 2010 by an immigration judge in Memphis, Tennessee.

Authorities in Belgium are restricting the freedom of Jewish private schools and home schoolers. One of the largest Jewish schools in the country, the Jesode Hatora School in Antwerp, is (at the time of writing in 2017) at risk of losing its state recognition and subsidies for being 'too conservative.'

Principals of schools in Victoria, Australia, have decided to axe Religious Instruction (RI) from their schools. Cathy Byrne, a sociology tutor, claims that her 'research has highlighted the divisive implications of RI curriculums that are racist, sexist, anti-science, age-inappropriate or somehow objectionable — even to church-going Christians.' Despite the rise of fundamentalist Islamic schools and the reluctance of the Australian authorities to take a firm approach to the teaching of Islam in Australia, Byrne portrays teaching of Christianity in schools as a public hazard. 'Whether we recognise it or not, whether we develop policies to address it or not, Christian religious extremism can be a security risk, a risk to the nature of our pluralist democracy and our hard-won liberal freedoms.'

NARRATIVE SUGGESTING SAME-SEX COUPLES MAKE BETTER PARENTS

Destruction of conventional family structures is the ultimate agenda of homosexual activism. The LGBT movement has exploited the ideal of the natural family and traditional marriage to validate its unconventional lifestyle.

It has won the battle for hearts and minds in the West through the media, Hollywood and popular culture. The most inoffensive tool of infiltrating popular culture is the American TV situation comedy, where the gay lifestyle is portrayed as fun, adventurous, romantic, and liberating. *Modern Family*, a popular sitcom, offers 'visibility' to a gay couple and thus legitimizes homosexual behaviour as normal and acceptable, says actor Eric Stonestreet — who plays one of the gay partners in the sitcom.

The state recognition of same-sex marriage has meant that gay couples can now adopt children in most Western countries. A disproportionately favourable narrative now dominates the portrayal of gay parenting. Thus, gay parents are viewed as not just acceptable, but demonstrably better than heterosexual couples in parenting skills and an ideal of love, stability and progressive parenting. Gay parents supposedly promote the healthy development of freethinking children who are free of the influence of backward, bigoted religious extremist parents.

In 1999, a key article in *American Psychologist* provoked public outrage because it challenged the essential role of the father in a family. In their study 'Deconstructing the Essential Father,' Silverstein and Auerbach contended that successful parenting is not gender specific and that children do not need fathers, or even mothers, but any gender configuration of adults could parent effectively.

A decade later, another study conducted by Biblarz and Stacey in 2010 entitled 'How does the Gender of Parents Matter?' and published in the *Journal of Marriage and the Family* pushed this to the limits insisting that 'two women parent better on average than a woman and a man,' i.e. lesbian parents were better parents than heterosexual parents. 'Lesbian co-parents seem to outperform comparable married heterosexual biological parents on several measures, even while being denied the substantial privileges of marriage,' they argue. 'Contrary to popular belief, studies have not shown that "compared to all other family forms, families headed by married, biological parents are best for children,"' is their surprising conclusion. The standards to determine good or bad parenting used by Biblarz and Stacey are revealing. For example, they claim that lesbian parents set less strict limits on their children, are less harsh with regards to discipline, show more respect for their children's independence, are more aware of what's going on their children's lives, are more open to acceptance of gender choice and sexual orientation and diversity and show more 'warmth, affection and attachment.' They also state that 'growing up without a father did not impede masculine development but enabled boys to achieve greater gender flexibility' (Biblarz & Stacey, 2010), thus indicating that children of lesbian parents are more likely to choose to become homosexual, bisexual or transgender.

The media have sensationalised this research without examining its methodology and bias, or reporting on other studies that contradict its findings. In 2014, *The Washington Times* ran a story with the bold headline 'Big Surprise: Gay parents give kids better "general health" says scientific report by gay dad.' The article supported a study conducted by Simon Crouch from the University of Melbourne, who is himself a gay parent. (Crouch, et al., 2014). Crouch claimed that his study — which researched 315 mostly lesbian parents — was the largest of its kind in the world (Crouch, 2014). He concluded that one of the main reasons for higher happiness in households run by gay parents is that housework is distributed more fairly.

Crouch's Australia-based study is methodologically flawed and such a serious deficiency skews the report's conclusions. Crouch admits that there is 'some bias' in the report and that the selection of the sample might make his 'analysis statistically underpowered.' The study used a self-selected 'convenience sample,' indicating that the respondents knew the purpose of the survey, and thus the political and social importance of the results, before they were asked to participate. Parents also mostly filled in the responses. Where children (between the ages of 10 and 17) responded, they did so in the presence their parents, although it would appear that the children's responses were not actually included in the results.

Crouch's study is flawed because 'it does not ask a representative sample of parents. It does not ask children independently of their parents. And it uses a method that is bound to show same-sex parents "on their best behaviour",' writes Carolyn Moynihan in her article, 'Not so fast: That Australian study on gay parenting tells us almost nothing useful.' 'Simply put, its participants are likely very aware of the political import of the study topic, and an unknown number of them probably signed up for that very reason,' adds Mark Regnerus, Associate Professor of Sociology at the University of Texas at Austin.

In 2016, two courageous scholars who were brought up by lesbian parents decided to expose the junk science and the fabricated mythology supporting the poisonous narrative of same-sex parenting. Robert Oscar Lopez and Brittany Klein described the children of same-sex parents as victims of child abuse. Their book *Jephthah's Children: The Innocent Casualties of Same-Sex Parenting* (2016) is an anthology of first-person accounts from children who were brought up by same-sex parents. The essays 'demonstrate how children's most fundamental birthright — the right to their mother and father, indeed their heritage — has been cast to the flames to make a small gay lobby happy....' 'As a child of same-sex parents it appears to me that our parents greatest sin is that they worshipped pleasure above all other gods,' writes Alana Newman, one of the witnesses in the book.

'A same-sex marriage between two men has no right to demand or even expect to be provided with other people's children,' sums up Klein. 'That requires a denial of children's basic human rights. Nobody has a "right" to children.... Children have the right to be born free, not bought or sold. They have a right to a mother and a father. Gay parenting is toxic to these rights,' she explains.

Lopez affirms this by arguing that 'the entire rationale behind gay marriage and gay parenting is that homosexuals have rights that they do not need to justify to other people. Despite the fact that copious statistics show that homosexual relationships have higher rates of instability, domestic violence, and emotional abuse, advocates for gay marriage still claim that they should have a right to marry because it is an entitlement that isn't subject to the approval or endorsement of other people, even experts. Yet what is the attitude shown toward kids who are forced to live in same-sex couple homes? The key word is 'forced,' because no child ends up in a gay home unless adults have taken extraordinary measures to place the child under the power of at least one, and possibly two, people who are not biologically related to him and therefore have no genetic or conceptual relationship to it.'

TO ABOLISH THE FAMILY IS TO DESTROY SOCIETY

In the last century, the eminent Oxford ethnologist and social anthropologist Joseph Unwin embarked on extensive research to prove that monogamous marriage and the family was an irrelevant and harmful institution. After studying 80 primitive tribes and six known civilizations through 5,000 years of history, Unwin discovered precisely the opposite of what he had hoped. The massive data revealed a positive correlation between the cultural achievement of a people and the sexual restraint they observe. In *Sex and Culture* (1934), he elaborated on his findings and concluded that only marriage with fidelity, what he called 'absolute monogamy,' would lead to the cultural prosperity of a society. On the other hand, the loosening of sexual restraints and the breakdown of the family would have calamitous consequences for society that would become evident in the third generation.

The savage assault in the West on marriage and the family can be traced to its roots in Marxism. Both Karl Marx and Friedrich Engels believed that a period of sexual promiscuity without families existed in the earliest period of human history. In *The German Ideology* Marx and Engels asserted, 'It is not possible to speak of "the" family.' 'Blessed is he who has no family,' Marx half-jokingly wrote to Engels. Marx and Engels blamed the family for the rise of private property and the division of labour, with women and children becoming the slaves of men.

Almost a century later, Marx's ideological descendants of the Frankfurt School would use 'critical theory' to deconstruct the very concept of the family. In his book *Eros and Civilization* (1955), Herbert Marcuse called for the celebration of 'polymorphous perversity.' Marcuse critiqued the idea of love as fundamentally repressive, guilt-inducing, and impossible, and argued for a liberation of perverse sexual desire.

If you can call any arrangement a family — never mind if it is two men, two women, or a polygamous arrangement — the word family has completely lost its meaning. Once advocates of gay marriage succeed in smashing the traditional definition of marriage and redefining it as no longer restricted to one man and one woman, they will continue to redefine it until it has no definition left.

Masha Gessen, author and gay activist, admitted to this agenda in a radio interview, 'It's a no-brainer that [homosexuals] should have the right to marry, but I also think equally that it's a no-brainer that the institution of marriage should not exist.... Fighting for gay marriage generally involves lying about what we are going to do with marriage when we get there — because we lie that the institution of marriage is not going to change, and it should change. And again, I don't think it should exist.' 'Being queer means pushing the parameters of sex, sexuality, and family, and, in the process, transforming the very fabric of society,' said Paula Ettelbrick, former legal director of Lambda Legal Defense and Education Fund.

Disastrously, even the Church has fallen prey to such warped reasoning. The year 2016 saw the 140th anniversary of the Mothers' Union, an organisation that was built on the solid rock of the Biblical ideal of family. Justin Welby, Archbishop of Canterbury, preached in his sermon on the occasion of this anniversary that the idea of a Victorian golden age of traditional family values was a 'myth.' The 'myth' of stable Victorian values was 'just that — mythology.' Welby, the spiritual leader of 85 million Anglicans, told an international gathering of women from the Mothers' Union that they had to face up to modern day society where divorce and same-sex couples are the norm.

When he was Chief Rabbi of the United Hebrew Congregations of the Commonwealth, Sir Jonathan Sacks described the maniacal destruction of the family. 'Today, we have divorced sex from love; love from commitment; commitment from marriage; marriage from having children; and having children from bearing responsibility for nurturing them and bringing them up. It is as if somebody had planted a bomb in the very midst of our most sacred institution and all we have left is fragments.'

7
THE MARGINALISATION OF CHRISTIANITY

CHRISTIANOPHOBIA

The West is not merely passively post-Christian and indifferent to Christianity; it is now actively anti-Christian and profoundly intolerant of the Christian faith.

George Yancey and David Williamson believe that the West is moving into Christianophobia, a state of fear and hatred against Christianity and Christians. In their book *So Many Christians, So Few Lions* (2015), they conduct what they believe to be the only academic enquiry of American scholars and their views on Christians and Christianity. Below are some of their findings.

> "I want them all to die in a fire," said one man with a doctorate. "I would be in favour of establishing a state for them.... If not then sterilize them so they can't breed more," said a middle-aged man with a master's degree. "The only good Christian is a dead Christian," said another under-45-year-old man with

a doctorate. "I abhor them and I wish we could do away with them," said a middle-aged woman with a master's degree. "A tortuous death would be too good for them," said a college-educated man between the ages of 36 and 45. "They should be eradicated without hesitation or remorse," said an elderly woman with a master's degree. "Restrict their ability to become judges, senators, representatives, member of Cabinet, military Chief of Staff and other powerful members of government," said a man over 75 with a bachelor's degree. "Should not be able to make decisions regarding the law, they should somehow have to be supervised if they are working with other people (drastic, I know)," said a woman under 45 with a master's degree. "We should put in place mandatory extreme prison sentences for anyone or any group that attempts to take away civil liberties guaranteed by our constitution," said a middle-aged man with a master's degree. "Churches should not be allowed to provide orphanages and adoption programs," said one elderly man with a doctorate. "I think we should restrict the indoctrination of children in religious dogma and ritual," said a middle-aged man with a master's degree. Conservative Christians should "not be allowed to hold political office, be police etc., serve in the armed forces," said another middle-aged man with a doctorate.

Christianity in the West is facing its most vicious attack from the postmodern 'cultured despisers of religion.' Over decades, the church has been progressively marginalised, but now basic Christian beliefs are even being criminalised. Western governments are aggressively passing new laws that limit the most fundamental freedoms of religion and speech and affect the rights of Christians to preach, evangelise, and hold to orthodox beliefs in the areas of marriage and sexuality. Despite living in allegedly free and democratic countries within the Western world, the church is encountering a rising tide of persecution. Western Christians admittedly do not face state-sponsored violence in the way that so many of their fellow-Christians do in other parts of the world. The level of violence — actual and threatened — that they do face is low but real, as we shall see later in this chapter. Yancey, Professor of Sociology at the

University of North Texas, explains that Western Christians are better off because those facing anti-Christian hostility are still a minority amongst Western Christians; but they should be concerned, because the sections of society infected with Christianophobia tend to be powerful elites with influence in certain important areas, such as higher education. The Christianophobes are also prominent in government and the judiciary and so the targeting of Christians is probably systemic and intentional. New laws and policies indicate that the situation is worsening. Each day, it is becoming more difficult to hold Christian views based on the Bible without fear of legal or social reprisals or vilification in the mainstream media or on social media.

LEGAL STRUCTURES

Although countries in the Western world each have their own legal framework and constitution, there are striking parallels marking the emerging anti-Christian trends.

After the Second World War, the shock and horror of the atrocities committed by the Nazis against the Jews compelled many Western nations to introduce laws aimed at eliminating hatred and violence based on ethnicity and religion. These laws were intended to guard against the virus of anti-Semitism that led to the Holocaust and to ensure that such a monumental crime against humanity would never again be committed against Jewish people or any other group. Over the years and with the rise of the women's rights and civil rights movements, Western nations passed laws to include other groups facing discrimination based on gender, colour and race. More recently, as more and more minority groups claim victim status, governments have passed more and more legislation banning discrimination against people on the grounds of race, gender, pregnancy, marital status, ethnic or social origin, colour, age, disability, religion, conscience, belief, culture, language, birth, trade and sexual orientation.

At first glance, such laws appear noble and commendable. They profess to promote equality, tolerance, and non-discrimination. Indeed, new legislation has been effective in protecting the rights of minority groups across the Western world, in contrast to many other countries where the rights of women and religious minorities are trampled upon. However, the avalanche of legislation under the heading of 'human rights' is now increasingly open to abuse, subjective interpretation and in many cases is in clear conflict with other freedoms enjoyed in democratic countries such as the freedoms of religion and expression.

To understand the impact such laws are having on Christianity, it is important to begin by discussing some general principles. Laws specific to protecting minority groups in most countries generally fall into three main categories.

Discrimination
Anti-discrimination law is intended to protect the right of all people to be treated equally. It mandates that policies and practices pertaining to participation in society – such as employment, buying or consuming goods and services, organisational membership and political membership – should allow equal participation and treatment regardless of group or identity characteristics such as race, religion, gender, disability, or sexual orientation. In addition, facilities and infrastructure, as much as is practicably reasonable, must be equally accessible to all people. Specific examples of unlawful discrimination could be refusing to employ someone because they were pregnant, refusing to serve someone at a restaurant because they were black, or refusing to provide disabled facilities at a shopping centre. Such discrimination is inexcusable and deplorable. However, supporters of such forms of human rights legislation run into serious difficulties with the issue of competing rights. According to the Ontario Human Rights Commission, competing human rights 'involve situations where parties to a dispute claim that the enjoyment of an individual or group's human rights and freedoms, as protected by law, would interfere with another's rights and freedoms.' What happens when the right of a religious group to practise their religion competes with the right of another minority group to be accorded equal treatment? Is there a hierarchy of rights in which, for example, the rights of sexual minorities trump the rights of religious minorities? Is it fair and just

when churches, Christian organisations and individual Christians are forced by competing laws to do something against their core beliefs?

Hate Crime

The term 'hate crime' was first used by three American Democrat politicians, John Conyers, Barbara Kennelly, and Mario Biaggi, in 1985 when they co-sponsored a bill in the House of Representatives entitled, 'Hate Crime Statistics Act.' The bill required the Department of Justice to collect and publish statistics on the nature and number of crimes motivated by racial, religious, and ethnic prejudice. It became popular when the author John Leo used it to challenge a law proposed by the District of Columbia which increased the sentence for criminal conduct motivated by prejudice. In his article entitled, 'The Politics of Hate' in the 9 October 1989 issue of *U.S. News and World Report*, Leo asked if a white person mugging a black person and delivering a slur was a greater crime than an ordinary mugging with a slur attached to it. 'If the skulls of all Americans are equally valuable (i.e. if this is a democracy), why not give everyone [the same sentence] for cracking any cranium at all?' he asked.

The UK's official police and legal definition of hate crime depends on the perception of the victim or of any other person.

Any criminal offence which is perceived by the victim or any other person to be motivated by hostility or prejudice based on a person's race or perceived race; religion or perceived religion; sexual orientation or perceived sexual orientation; disability or perceived disability and any crime motivated by hostility or prejudice against a person who is transgender or perceived to be transgender. (Crown Prosecution Service)

Hate crimes range from beating up someone just because they are Asian to painting swastikas on Jewish graves, and from breaking into a mosque to desecrate it with a pig's head to men inflicting 'corrective rape' on a lesbian in order to change her sexuality. Such behaviour is detestable and abhorrent. Christians must stand firmly against all forms of prejudice and hatred.

The problem with the category of hate crime is obvious from the above Crown Prosecution Service's definition which hinges on the word 'perceived.' Hatred or prejudice is rendered entirely subjective and depends on the perception of the victim. The problem is further complicated by the definition of 'hate.' As columnist Jules Gomes writes in *The Conservative Woman*, 'Hate is a feeling, an emotion of "intense dislike" of someone. It may result in an act, but it is not an act. Even if hatred is understood as prejudice, prejudice is thinking ill of a person or certain groups of people. It may result in an act, but it is not an act. The law can only judge acts, not feelings or thoughts. If the act is illegal anyway, to punish the offender's prejudices or feelings behind the commission of the crime is to punish emotions or thought.'

Gomes also identifies a moral problem with hate crime. 'Morally, are we to criminalise a hierarchy of motives? Is killing someone with the motive of jealousy more evil than killing someone with a racist motive? Why is prejudicial hatred more morally reprehensible than hatred for jealousy or greed? ... By privileging victim status we are saying that people belonging to some groups are more valuable than others and those not belonging to these groups are somehow less deserving of similar protection under the law.'

'The current anti-hate crime movement is generated not by an epidemic of unprecedented bigotry but by heightened sensitivity to prejudice and, more important, by our society's emphasis on identity politics,' write James Jacobs and Kimberly Potter in a hard-hitting treatise *Hate Crimes: Criminal Law and Identity Politics*. Jacobs and Potter argue for abolishing the category of hate crime.

Hate Speech
Hate speech is any expression (spoken or written), image or gesture made privately or publicity that promotes or incites hatred or aggression towards a certain group or individual based on group attributes. Even though hate speech may incite violence, the legal parameters of the definition are constantly being widened to include any speech that may be perceived by victim groups to be insulting, vilifying or hateful. The problem lies in identifying what may be perceived as hateful.

Hate speech has no place within the church. It is diametrically opposed to the most important teaching of our Lord Jesus to love one's neighbour and even one's enemy. However, should a secular government legislate against what is hateful? In the Old Testament, Israel had laws against hatred. 'Do not hate a fellow Israelite in your heart. Rebuke your neighbour frankly so you will not share in their guilt' (Leviticus 19:17). The law code of Deuteronomy goes even further. It commands the Israelites not to hate two groups of people who were enemies of Israel. 'You must not hate an Edomite, for he is your relative; you must not hate an Egyptian, for you lived as a foreigner in his land' (Deuteronomy 23:7 NET Bible).

Ancient Israel could legislate on hate because it was a theocracy. The Mosaic Law was civil, criminal, ritual — all put together in a society where no distinction was made between sacred and secular and every aspect of life was brought under the jurisdiction of the God of Abraham. In the New Testament 'hate' does not have the force of state legislation. 'Anyone who claims to be in the light but hates a brother or sister is still in the darkness,' writes the apostle John (1 John 2:9). To hate someone is now a sin and no longer a violation of state law. 'It is only religion in a theocracy that has the authority to legislate on hate (or love). For a secular state to pass legislation on hate crime is for it to usurp the role of the divine and to play God, demanding total allegiance of thought and feeling; heart, mind and soul. In a post-Christian society that has lost the religious category of sin and has no religious imperatives to regulate sinful thoughts, feelings, and emotions of hate and prejudice, secular law is taking the place of religion. This is idolatry at its worst,' observes Gomes.

FREE SPEECH VS HATE SPEECH

How does one determine what is hate speech? Andrew Sellars, a director of Boston University School of Law, has examined various laws and definitions of hate speech across the world, as well those used by social media giants like Facebook and Twitter. He begins his 2012 *Law Review* article entitled 'Defining Hate Speech' with these words:

Few pairs of words evoke such a diverse range of feelings, perspectives, and reactions as "hate speech." Calls are made for it to be embraced, tolerated, ridiculed, targeted for counter-speech, blocked on websites, actionable in a civil lawsuit, made criminally illegal, or the basis of war crimes prosecution, with no shortage of shading in between.

He concludes

I have laboured through many definitions and examined their theoretical shortcomings. All of this may feel as though I am trying to work scholars and regulators to such a confused place that they refuse to study hate speech altogether. This is not my intent at all. I only seek to illustrate that this is difficult, it is difficult for good reason in light of the competing interests at play, and we should approach these questions in an intelligent manner. A person who says they have an easy solution to the problem of hate speech, or even how to observe and document hate speech, is simply not thinking hard enough.

Many contend that hate speech is not merely difficult, but almost impossible to define. Jacob Mchangama, in his excellent paper 'The Problem with Hate Speech Laws' published in *The Review of Faith and International Affairs* journal (2015), sums up the argument well.

There are strong reasons to question the inclusion of hate speech bans in international human rights law. First, the drafting history of international anti-hate speech laws shows that such laws are a legacy of totalitarian states aimed at abusing human rights rather than strengthening tolerance. Second, the applicable standards are conflicting, impossible to reconcile with the principle of legal certainty inherent in the rule of law, and prone to abuses that undermine critically important freedoms of speech — especially political speech. Third, laws against hate speech and against "offense" are tools in the hands of those who would severely restrict religious freedom. Finally, proponents of hate speech bans have yet to demonstrate convincingly any link between such bans and social peace and tolerance.

A vigorous contest is raging between free speech and hate speech. Criticism, protest, satire and difference of opinion is increasingly deemed hateful by certain groups. Causing offence is viewed as causing harm.

What constitutes hate or abuse or offence is highly subjective. What one group considers sacred, orthodox, or central to their identity may be seen as dangerous, damaging and detrimental by another group. One person's free speech is another person's hate speech.

The European Court of Human Rights makes it clear that the right to free speech, 'is applicable not only to "information" or "ideas" that are favourably received or regarded as inoffensive or as a matter of indifference, but also to those that offend, shock or disturb the State or any sector of the population.' In the US, the First Amendment protects the right to free speech, even if it is offensive.

British comedian and satirist, Rowan Atkinson, is vehemently opposed to hate speech laws being enforced by the state as this could limit the use of satire as a form of social commentary. 'The clear problem of the outlawing of insult is that too many things can be interpreted as such. Criticism, ridicule, sarcasm, merely stating an alternative point of view to the orthodoxy, can be interpreted as insult.' Rowan Atkinson (2012)

In addition, the threshold of what constitutes discrimination and hate crimes or hate speech is becoming lower and lower. Inciting people to cause hateful actions and violence has been replaced with merely causing offence. Lisa Feldman Barrett, a Professor of Psychology at Northeastern University, stretches the idea of hate speech to the very limits and is adamant that abusive words can cause direct physical harm. In a column for the *New York Times*, she writes that 'Words can have a powerful effect on your nervous system. Certain types of adversity, even those involving no physical contact, can make you sick, alter your brain — even kill neurons — and shorten your life.' She draws a distinction between conservative provocateur Milo Yiannopoulos and conservative academic Charles Murray, arguing that Yiannopoulos's lectures on university campuses should be banned because they are abusive, while Murray's lectures are offensive and should be challenged through debate but not banned.

In some countries, the law does not even require a specific injured party; someone else may claim that someone of a particular identity group may have been offended or harmed by another's viewpoint or expression. Offence can be real or merely probable.

There are countries where corroboration is not required. Someone may bring a charge without proof. It is difficult to measure offence; actions are much more quantifiable. Some legal systems place the burden of proof on the accused rather than the accuser; hence it is up to the accused to prove that their statements or actions were not hate speech rather than for the complainant to prove that they were.

Advocate Nadene Badenhorst of Freedom of Religion South Africa organisation, stated that the Hate Crimes and Hate Speech Bill (2016) introduced in South Africa, 'criminalises just about any communication (in the broadest sense of the word) that any person or group may potentially not like, disagree with or find offensive.' If the bill were to be passed, she said, it would muzzle believers of all religions 'from preaching, teaching or speaking "controversial" Scriptures and issues like abortion, creationism, euthanasia, prostitution, sexual immorality, etc. for fear that they will become a target of liberal activists who will no doubt use the Bill to push their own agenda and silence, in their opinion, "extremist, fundamentalist, narrow-minded and bigoted" views.'

Badenhorst describes what life would be like if the bill becomes law: 'No one would dare open their mouths for fear that someone might take offence and report them to the authorities. Debate on issues such as what is morally right and wrong, what is just and unjust, would be shut down and the very freedoms we cherish as South Africans, namely free speech and freedom of religion, would be reined in.'

THE SILENCING OF CHRISTIAN BELIEF

A tidal wave of restrictive legislation is battering the church and orthodox Christians who find themselves slapped with penalties ranging from diversity and sensitivity training and fines to community service and prison. Other religious groups like Orthodox Jews are also affected, but Christianity in particular provides a soft target and is specifically the focus of much hate speech legislation. In liberal and secular societies, a variety of viewpoints and lifestyles are in open conflict with the most basic teachings of the Bible. Christians are now increasingly prevented from expressing views or practising their faith in a number of areas.

The uniqueness of Christ

The Bible teaches that the only way to salvation is through Jesus Christ. We believe that followers of other religions are unfortunately mistaken or deceived. Salvation is by grace alone through faith alone and a person who is not saved is lost for all eternity. Sharing the good news of salvation with people of other religions (or none) to save them from certain eternal torment in hell, is an imperative and rooted in the Great Commission of our Lord Jesus Christ. This belief cannot avoid clashing with other religious beliefs and worldviews who offer a different way to salvation. However, such a view is condemned as exclusive, intolerant and hateful.

It must be pointed out that all religions make exclusive claims that are in conflict with the claims of other religions. Christians believe that Jesus alone is God's final revelation, while Muslims believe that God's revelation through Jesus is not final but has been superseded by God's revelation through Muhammad, who is the final revelation of God. Both claims are exclusive and irreconcilable. It is no small irony that secular ideologies make exclusive claims with the same religious fervour and dogmatism! Communism believes in the abolition of private property, while capitalism believes that private property is absolute.

The sanctity of life

Christianity holds that life is sacred and God-given and must be protected. This is in direct conflict with pro-choice beliefs, which promote abortion as a fundamental human right, and its corollary in the form of assisted suicide or euthanasia. Christian who stand for the rights of the unborn child are caricatured as anti-women and anti-choice. Christians who stand against euthanasia are derided as people who enjoy watching others suffer. Christian doctors, nurses and other medical professionals are particular targets since they are offered little or no choice to opt out of medical procedures that blatantly contradict their most cherished values and are often forced to conduct such procedures against their conscience and belief.

The binary nature of gender

Christians believe that God created humans male and female, and that each human is either male or female (Genesis 1:27). There are very rare instances where genetic dysfunction results in cases of intersex. However, secular society is widely embracing the idea of gender fluidity and affirms that people can now choose their own gender. There are multiple gender identities (Facebook lists over 50 gender options). Even though less than one percent of children experience gender dysphoria, which has been recognized as a mental disorder, governments are endorsing transgenderism as a viable option and children are given a choice to undergo hormone therapy and gender transitioning surgery. In its July 2017 General Synod, the Church of England passed a shocking resolution in favour of creating specially designed 'baptism-like' liturgies to welcome people who had undergone gender transitioning under their new gender identity. There is a growing push by transgender groups for access to public toilets and changing rooms according to their chosen rather than their birth gender. Many, especially women and children, have said that they feel extremely vulnerable, uncomfortable and at risk using toilets and changing rooms with someone of the opposite sex. However, voicing such concern could be interpreted as hate speech. In June 2017, the province of Ontario, Canada, passed a law that allows the government to remove the child from its parents if the parents use the child's biological gender pronoun, rather than the child's preferred one. An overwhelming majority of 63 to 23 legislators in the Ontario legislature voted in favour of the law called 'The Supporting Children, Youth and Families Act.'

The nature of homosexual practice

Western society not only accepts same-sex sexual relations but celebrates and validates them with laws allowing same-sex marriage and same-sex parents to adopt children. LGBT groups, who believe any criticism of homosexual behaviour is tantamount to a hate crime, have gone out of their way to trap and target conservative Christians. Many mainline denominations have fallen captive to the LGBT agenda and now have liturgies for blessing same-sex couples or even marrying them in church. On the one hand, LGBT activists maintain that gender is fluid. On the other hand, they believe that sexual orientation is fixed. Therefore, any attempt to change a person's sexual behaviour, even if a homosexual chooses to leave his or her lifestyle, is considered a hate crime. The July 2017 Synod of the Church of England, mentioned above, also passed a resolution by an overwhelming majority banning 'conversion therapy' — even if it meant no more than praying for a homosexual person who had freely and without coercion expressed a desire to 'convert' to a heterosexual life.

The sanctity of marriage

Since its inception the Church has upheld the Biblical ideal of a lifelong monogamous marriage between a man and a woman. The institution of marriage is so exalted that the Old Testament likened the relationship between Yahweh and Israel to a marriage. Similarly, the New Testament drew on this metaphor to express the bond between Christ and His Church. Christians view sex as God's good gift to be consummated and celebrated within the covenant of holy matrimony. A person who is living habitually and unrepentantly in a sexual relationship outside marriage is living in sin. This is one of the most counter-cultural teachings of the church in the postmodern West, since living together before marriage or cohabitation without any desire to get married has become the norm.

The symbols that provoke scandal

The symbol of the cross has always been at the heart of Christian faith and practice. Christians have also prayed in public at various hours of the day. In Europe, state churches encouraged prayer even in settings of local and central government. Chaplains are appointed to the armed forces, universities, hospitals, prisons and even to Parliament. However, there have been virulent attacks against any public display of Christian symbols or services and the ministry of chaplaincy is increasingly being downgraded to that of a glorified social worker.

It is important to distinguish between individuals and ideas. People must always be protected from harm and allowed to express their beliefs freely, but the beliefs themselves should not be protected from analysis, critique and criticism. The protection of people is vitally important for they are all created in the image of God and carry His dignity and therefore should never be insulted, abused, vilified or attacked. No matter how much we may disagree with a person's beliefs, ideology or practice, Christians must never attack the person; indeed they must be willing to protect that person when attacked by others, to support that person when vilified, and to stand alongside them, despite their difference of belief. This is part of the Christian command to live a life of love (Ephesians 5:2). The criminalisation of homosexual practice is completely unacceptable, as is the criminalisation of opinions disagreeing with homosexual practice; any judgement must be left to God.

LEGAL CASES AND LAWS MARGINALISING CHRISTIANITY IN THE WEST

A small sample of some of the many recent cases of Christians being victimised for their beliefs will show the ominous development of the legal marginalisation of Christianity. Christians are facing a swelling tide of legal judgements against them. The Bible is in effect being censored as laws and legal judgements against reading, teaching or displaying sections of the Bible are passed. Christian parents are prevented from adopting or fostering children if they hold Biblical views on homosexuality. There are now multiple cases of unfair employment discrimination based on the traditional view of sexuality. Christians are not even allowed to express their conviction that Jesus is the only way to salvation. Irish pastor James McConnell, who was charged with a 'hate crime motive,' said:

> The police tried to shut me up and tell me what to preach. It's ridiculous. I believe in freedom of speech. I'm going to keep on preaching the gospel. I have nothing against Muslims, I have never hated Muslims. I have never hated anyone. But I am against what Muslims believe. They have the right to say what they believe in and I have a right to say what I believe.

Sweden 2003
In 2002, Sweden passed a hate speech bill, which explicitly took account of 'church sermons' as subject to hate speech restrictions. Sweden's parliament, the Riksdag, released a statement at the passing of the bill asserting that church sermons which characterise homosexual behaviour as sinful 'might' be considered a criminal offence. A year later, Pentecostal pastor Ake Green was arrested and found guilty of hate speech for preaching against homosexuality in a sermon and using Bible verses to support his statements. Green spent a month in prison. Prosecutor Kjell Yngvesson, justified Pastor Green's sentence saying, 'One may have whatever religion one wishes, but this is an attack on all fronts against homosexuals. Collecting Bible citations on this topic as he does makes this hate speech.'

United Kingdom 2007
Foster parents Vincent and Pauline Matherick, had their foster child taken away and placed in a hostel, because they refused to sign sexual equality regulations as part of the foster parents contract. According to the contract, foster parents are required to discuss same-sex relationships with children as young as eleven. They have to teach foster children that same-sex partnerships are as acceptable as heterosexual partnerships, and they have to expose their children to LGBTI association meetings. The Mathericks, who had fostered 30 children over many years, were taken off the foster care list. It was only

after a legal battle that the Mathericks were fully reinstated as foster parents by Somerset County Council in May 2008.

Australia 2010

In 2010, Australia began implementing the Safe School programme, which aims to 'set a baseline of understanding about the matters impacting on LGBTI students ....' Lee Jones, a Christian IT specialist from Melbourne, was tasked with working on part of the programme. He was asked by his manager how he felt about the programme. Jones stated that he would work on the project but had some religious concerns. In particular, he would not want his own children to be taught some of the more controversial elements of the programme especially in relation to gender fluidity and sexuality. He was dismissed for 'creating an unsafe work environment.'

United States 2013

In 2013, florist Barronelle Stutzman from Washington State was ordered to pay a large fine and legal expenses for refusing to providing flowers for a same-sex wedding because of her belief that marriage should be between a man and a woman. The court ruled:

> We therefore hold that the conduct for which Stutzman was cited and fined in this case — refusing her commercially marketed wedding floral services to Ingersoll and Freed because theirs would be a same-sex wedding — constitutes sexual orientation discrimination.

European Court of Human Rights 2013

Three British Christians who claimed that their religious rights were violated by employers took their cases to the European Court of Human Rights.

Shirley Chaplin, a nurse in the UK's National Health Service, was not allowed to wear a cross around her neck in front of patients. She was transferred to a desk job when she refused to take off her cross. The European Grand Chamber ruled in favour of the NHS decision. Strangely, Nadia Eweida, a British Airways employee who was dismissed from her job for refusing to remove her cross, and who lost her case of unfair dismissal in the British courts, had won her case on appeal in Europe earlier in 2013. This allowed her to return to work and wear her cross.

Marriage registrar Lillian Ladele was disciplined by Islington Council in London for refusing to conduct civil partnerships ceremonies between same-sex couples. The European Court of Human Rights ruled that she could not refuse services based on conscience or religious convictions as it would be discrimination on the grounds of sexual orientation.

Gary McFarlane, a counsellor for the charity Relate was dismissed for indicating that he had a conscientious objection to providing relationship therapy to same-sex couples. McFarlane was found to be guilty of discrimination and his dismissal was upheld as fair.

Keith Porteous Wood, Executive Director of the National Secular Society, comments on the judgements.

> Fortunately, Europe's highest court has now wisely followed numerous lower courts and rejected the applicants' attempts for religious conscience to trump equality law.... The UK has the world's most comprehensive equality laws which already include strong protection for religious believers and they would have been fatally compromised, particularly for LGBT (lesbian, gay, bisexual, trans-sexual) people had the Grand Chamber overturned any of these judgments. We hope that this will now draw a line under the attempts by a small coterie of Christian activists to obtain special privileges for themselves which would invariably come at the expense of other people's rights. The principle of equality for all, including for religious believers, is now established and they should stop wasting the time of the courts with these vexatious cases.

Sweden 2015
Swedish midwife Ellinor Grimmark objected to performing abortions. She was told by the Swedish Labour Court that she had to choose between conscience or career. She was unable to find employment

within Sweden because of her belief in the 'dignity of human life.' No clinic or hospital was prepared to hire her. In November 2015, a district court found that Grimmark's right to freedom of conscience had not been violated and required her to pay the local government legal fees of more than $100,000.

United States 2015

Aaron and Melissa Klein, owners of a family bakery in Oregon, were asked to bake a wedding cake for same-sex couple Rachel and Laurel Bowman-Cryer (whom they had served many times). The Kleins declined on religious grounds. They suffered severe social media abuse and a boycott and were taken to court. They lost their bakery and Aaron was forced to work as a garbage collector. The Kleins were fined $135,000 and ordered 'to cease and desist from publishing, circulating, issuing or displaying, or causing to be published ... any communication to the effect that any of the accommodations ... will be refused, withheld from or denied to, or that any discrimination be made against, any person on account of their sexual orientation.' This was essentially a 'gagging order.' If the Kleins decide to fight the ruling, they could be fined again.

Northern Ireland 2015

James McConnell, an evangelical pastor, was charged with making 'grossly offensive' remarks about Islam during his sermon at the Whitewell Metropolitan Tabernacle in Belfast. In 2014, McConnell (then aged 77) had preached on 1 Timothy 2:5 'For there is one God, and one mediator between God and men, the man Christ Jesus.'

He went on to preach:

> The Muslim religion was created many hundreds of years after Christ. Mohammed was born in 570. But Muslims believe that Islam is the true religion, dating back to Adam, and that the biblical patriarchs were all Muslims, including Noah and Abraham and Moses, and even our Lord Jesus Christ.... To judge by some of what I have heard in the past few months, you would think that Islam was little more than a variation of Christianity and Judaism. Not so. Islam's ideas about God,

about humanity, about salvation are vastly different from the teachings of the Holy Scriptures. Islam is heathen. Islam is satanic. Islam is a doctrine spawned in Hell.

The Belfast Islamic Centre reported McConnell to the police who launched an investigation as to whether the sermon and the use of the Bible constituted a hate crime. After a protracted period of time and a media circus, the pastor was cleared of all charges by a judge at the Belfast Magistrates Court. District Judge Liam McNally said, 'The courts need to be very careful not to criticise speech which, however contemptible, is no more than offensive. It is not the task of the criminal law to censor offensive utterances.'

United States 2015
Fontbonne Academy, an all-girls Catholic school in Massachusetts, revoked their job offer of food caterer to Matthew Barrett, when they discovered that he was in a same-sex marriage. The judge stated:

> Fontbonne's discrimination 'because of' Barrett's same-sex marriage is undisputed and amounts to discriminatory intent as a matter of law.... It is clear that, because he is male, he suffered gender discrimination when he was denied employment for marrying a person whom a female could have married without suffering the same consequences.

The decision was criticised by the Catholic Action League of Massachusetts, which called it

> a frontal assault on religious freedom, an appalling subordination of the First Amendment to the Massachusetts gay rights law, and a victory by homosexual activists in their campaign to coerce Christians into compliance with same sex marriage.... Judge Wilkins's decision would compel Catholic institutions to hire those who reject and despise Catholic teaching, fatally impairing the constitutionally protected right of those institutions to carry on their mission.

This was the first time a court had sided against a religious institution in this regard in the United States.

Norway 2015

Devout Pentecostals Ruth and Maris Bodnariu had their five children forcibly removed from them after the parents were found guilty of 'Christian radicalism and indoctrination.' They appealed the decision but lost. The removal was triggered by the school principal who complained to child welfare services that the Bodnariu parents were 'very Christian' and their belief that God punishes sin 'creates a disability in the children.' The two oldest children were removed from school without their parents' knowledge. Later that day police arrived at the family home and took away the third and fourth children, leaving only the three-month-old baby, who was taken away the next day. The children were split up and placed in institutional care or with foster parents. The parents were allowed to visit their baby son twice a week for two hours, and to see their older sons occasionally, but they were not allowed to visit their two daughters.

Switzerland 2016

A Salvation Army nursing home in Switzerland was told that its staff must allow and even perform assisted suicides if requested or face losing their charitable status. The nursing home mounted a legal challenge and lost the case.

Australia 2016

An Adelaide university student was suspended in 2016 for offering to pray for another student who was stressed over her workload. He was asked about his views on homosexuality, to which he replied that he 'would treat any gay person kindly but did not agree with their choice.' He was suspended and ordered to undergo 're-education' classes for homophobia.

Belgium 2016

A Catholic nursing home in Diest was fined for refusing euthanasia to a terminally ill patient. Belgium has one of the world's most liberal laws on physician-assisted suicide, which is not just for the terminally ill. In practice, patients with psychiatric conditions — even children — can request euthanasia. Sint-Augustinus rest home was ordered to pay a total of €6,000 after it stopped doctors from giving a lethal injection to Mariette Buntjens. The patient's family sued the nursing home after her death a few days later, for causing their mother 'unnecessary mental and physical suffering.' A federal Belgian court fined the home more than €6,000. The judges who presided over the case ruled that 'the nursing home had no right to refuse euthanasia on the basis of conscientious objection.'

United Kingdom 2016

In July 2016, four Christian street preachers were arrested in Bristol City Centre and charged with using 'threatening or abusive behaviour within the hearing or sight of a person likely to be caused harassment, alarm or distress thereby.' Because of past harassment, one of the preachers wore a body camera which filmed both the preaching and the crowd of hecklers around them. Even though it was the hecklers and not the preachers who used foul and abusive language, Bristol Magistrates Court convicted two of the street preachers in February 2017, stating that the comments they made were offensive towards Islam and homosexuals. The preachers' defence lawyer provided an expert witness statement which pointed out that almost everything they said was directly quoted from the King James Bible. In other words, they were not making the comments themselves but rather quoting sections out of the Bible. However, the prosecution lawyer told the court that in the context of modern society this 'must be considered to be abusive and is a criminal matter.' The preachers were found not guilty at a re-trial in June 2017.

Australia 2016

A Christian civil servant in Victoria was given an official warning for objecting to being forced to take part in a gay pride march. He later asked to be taken off the government department's LGBTI network as he found the unsolicited emails were 'offensive by reason of his religious background.' He had to submit a notice to show why he should not be disciplined for asking to be taken off the LGBTI network email list. Eventually the investigation was dropped and no further action was taken against the civil servant.

United States 2017

In June 2017, the Illinois Department of Children and Family Services instituted a number of radical changes to its policies and procedures to cater for children who experience gender dysphoria. The policy now 'requires that all LGBTQ children and youth be placed in an affirming safe housing, receive LGBTQ competent medical and mental health services, and have equal opportunity and access to care.' Volunteers and caregivers, foster parents or prospective adoptive parents 'have to complete mandatory training in LGBTQ competency.' Foster parents or prospective adoptive parents are rejected if they believe in the Biblical teaching on sexuality and marriage. Mary Hasson of the Ethics and Public Policy Center in Washington D.C. commented on this new policy.

> Forget the democratic process. Forget free speech, freedom of religion, and the conscience rights of American citizens. Forget the welfare of vulnerable children. The state of Illinois heels to the commands of LGBTQ activists; it has embraced a new creed based on the LGBTQ vision of the human person. The only winners are progressive activists and lawyers eager to fill their litigation dockets. The losers? Illinois' most vulnerable children.

LGBTQQIP2SAA

The abbreviation LGBT for lesbian, gay, bisexual and transgender people is sometimes used with further initials added. A fairly common usage is LGBTQIA where Q stands for either 'queer' or 'questioning,' I stands for 'intersex' and A stands for either 'asexual' or 'allied,' that is, heterosexuals supportive of the LGBT community. Others add just I or just Q to the standard LGBT. Sometimes the + sign is used to indicate that there are more categories than have been listed.

If the initials of all the categories currently identified were included the abbreviation would run LGBTQQIP2SAA with P for 'pansexual' and 2S for 'Two-Spirit.'

Canada 2017

At the time of writing, a local government board in Alberta is trying to prevent the Cornerstone Christian Academy from teaching or displaying Bible passages that may be considered offensive to others. Battle River School Division (BRSD) chair, Lauri Skori, told Cornerstone's chair, Deanna Margel that 'any scripture that could be considered offensive to particular individuals should not be read or studied in school.' The school was also required to remove a Bible verse against immorality displayed on a wall.

In March 2017 a new motion, known as M 103, was passed by the Ottawa Parliament, which singled out Islam for special protection. It was tabled by a Muslim Member of Parliament, Iqra Khalid, who urged the government to condemn Islamophobia and to 'develop a whole of the government approach to reducing or eliminating systematic racism and religious discrimination including Islamophobia.' Despite a national poll indicating that 71% of the population would oppose the bill, it passed 201 to 91 in the legislature. Columnist Lorne Gunter wrote in the *Toronto Sun*:

> While purporting to oppose all forms of religious discrimination, the only form specifically mentioned is Islamophobia. And no definition of Islamophobia is given, leaving the door wide open to the broadest possible interpretations — including public statements condemning radical Islamic terrorism and even academic papers questioning whether Islam truly is a religion of peace.

New Zealand 2017

At the time of writing, Family First, a Christian charity which aims to 'promote and advance research and policy supporting marriage and family as foundational to a strong and enduring society' is under threat from the New Zealand Charities Registration Board, which is attempting to strip Family First of its charitable status. In August 2017, the Charities Registration Board said this was because Family First 'does not advance exclusively charitable purposes ...' but 'has a purpose to promote its own particular views about marriage and the traditional family that cannot be determined to be for the public benefit in a way previously accepted as charitable.' Family First affirms 'the natural family to be the union of a man and a woman through marriage' and insists that 'the natural family cannot change into some new shape; nor can it be re-defined by eager social engineers.' The Charities Registration Board had tried the same in 2015, but an appeal by Family First was allowed by the Wellington High Court.

SOCIETAL MARGINALISATION

Running parallel to the pressure Western Christians face from laws designed to suffocate their beliefs and behaviour is unofficial intimidation from society. The legal and societal coercion each reinforce the other, squeezing Christians into a position of retreat or surrender.

Chilling effect and double standards of the law in the West
Christianity in the West is subject to what is known, in legal terms, as a chilling effect. A chilling effect occurs when the threat of legal, or in some cases social, pressure acts to deter or discourage an individual or group from practising a constitutional right such as free speech. Christians now are extremely hesitant about what to say or how to act lest they be found guilty of discrimination or hate crimes. As we have seen above, instances of Christians no longer able to voice opinions, stand for issues of justice, adopt children, choose not to kill another person — whether an unborn baby or a sick or elderly adult — or even read or quote the Bible freely, are becoming more frequent in the West. A Barnabas Fund article entitled 'Hate Crime Is Becoming A Weapon To Use Against Christians' (2017) discussed the increased persecution of Christians in the West.

> Hate crime legislation needs to make a clear distinction between its proper role in protecting people and its misuse to silence criticism of beliefs or ideas. It must never be allowed to be used as a weapon to silence legitimate criticism of any belief or ideology, whether Christian, Islamic or humanist, however much that may offend the adherents of those beliefs.

Double standards abound when dealing with discrimination and anti-hate legislation. Government agencies are quick to react to often unfounded and frivolous cases against Christians accused of hate crimes. However, hate crime against Christians is ignored or dismissed despite prejudice or violence against Christians because of their faith. In December 2016, Barnabas Fund submitted evidence to an inquiry by the UK House of Commons Select Committee on Home Affairs substantiating this claim. The submission identified three types of anti-Christian violence in the UK.

- Acts of violence against Christians arising from a general contempt for Christians held by some sections of society. This is similar to some forms of anti-Semitism and anti-Muslim hatred.

- Threats and sometimes actual acts of violence carried out against Christians and Christian property by a minority of LGBT rights extremists. The arson and death threats received by the owners of Ashers Bakery in Northern Ireland, after they declined an order to bake a cake promoting the redefinition of marriage, are one example of such intimidation. In May 2015 they were found guilty at Belfast High Court of discrimination on the grounds of sexual orientation.

- Attempts at forced reconversion of Christians from Muslim backgrounds. Such attempts may involve illegal imprisonment for days, weeks or even months in a room or garage, extreme physical and emotional abuse, and attempts to lure the person overseas where they may be subjected to similar forms of 'persuasion' and/or forced marriage to a Muslim. Though such violence is widespread and organisations like Barnabas Fund had repeatedly raised it over many years, the UK Hate Crime Action Plan did not even mention it.

Europe's legal watchdog, The Legal Project, echoes the disquiet over the double standards so often seen in the application of hate crime legislation.

> Given the nebulous standards on which much of Europe's hate speech laws are based — indeed, there is not even a universally

agreed upon definition for what constitutes hate speech — it is little wonder that such legislation has ensnared speech it was likely never meant to punish. Delineating the line between speech that is considered rude and that which is considered insulting for the purposes of criminal prosecution is an utterly subjective undertaking, and a distinction that governments are ill-suited to determine. Compounding the problem of these laws' arbitrariness is their selective application: while European authorities have at times appeared reluctant to go after Islamist firebrands spouting hatred, those engaging in legitimate debate about Islamism are frequently targeted for prosecution.

Freedom of Religion South Africa cites a specific example.

Again, the double standard is shown in the case of Pastor André Bekker, a former homosexual who now leads a Christian organisation that ministers to people with unwanted same-sex attraction, and to families and loved ones of people with same-sex attraction. In this case, Bekker lodged a complaint with the SAHRC [South African Human Rights Commission] against a number of LGBT activists, complaining that their denial that a person is capable of changing their sexual orientation and effectively calling persons who have changed (including Bekker himself) 'liars,' amount to unfair discrimination and 'hate speech' against former homosexuals. The SAHRC rejected Bekker's complaint and his appeal, on the basis that the comments (by the LGBT activists), were 'merely expressed opinions in the ordinary course of debate, which comments fell within the ambit of the right to freedom of expression and therefore did not amount to hate speech.' However, when journalist Jon Qwelane expressed his opinion that 'gay is not okay' in the ordinary course of debate, the same SAHRC took him to the Equality Court for 'hate speech' in terms of PEPUDA! [Promotion of Equality and Prevention of Unfair Discrimination Act 2000]

THE WILTON PARK CONFERENCE REPORT

Wilton Park, an executive agency of the UK Foreign and Commonwealth Office (FCO), convened a meeting from 7-9 September 2016 on *Opportunities and Challenges: The intersection of faith and human rights of LGBTI+ persons.* The agency published a report after the conference which made a number of recommendations with implications for Christians in the UK and the Global South. The report is highly discriminatory specifically against Christianity. Actively promoting the LGBTI agenda, the report uses inflammatory language to describe Christian missionaries 'spreading prejudiced views,' contributing 'to the context in which these attitudes and behaviour have flourished' and entrenching 'hateful attitudes towards homosexuality, transgender and intersexuality.' Evangelical Christians are characterised as people who have 'intensified hatred, disseminating it in parts of the world which had previously exercised greater tolerance.' Biblical theology is disparaged as reflecting 'the heteropatriarchy of Christianity brought by western missionaries.' The report insinuates that churches who take a conservative view of homosexual acts are acting immorally, and therefore the state should discriminate against them. 'In situations when the state abdicates responsibility to provide services such as education or health, it also diminishes the ability to exercise moral authority against churches which are providing them.' It calls for the government to make it mandatory for churches and Christians to uphold LGBTI ideology or have their influence and ministries within sectors such as health and education revoked. Elsewhere, the report calls for 'direct action' instead of 'dialogue' against religious leaders and those opposed to the LGBTI lifestyle. This includes legal action, exposing the identity of opponents and mass mobilisation. The Wilton Park report makes a large number of other recommendations including government sponsored and regulated interpretations of the Bible, monitoring of church activity and imposing state-approved curricula within Sunday Schools to promote the LGBTI lifestyle to children as well as similar training in theological seminaries.

BLASPHEMY LAWS

Globalisation and social media have elevated managing hate speech and hate crime to the level of an international concern. In March 2017, the Pakistani government announced that it was working with 21 other Muslim-majority countries to introduce a global Islamic blasphemy law (i.e. prohibiting criticism of Islam) on social media. The new law envisages prosecuting people for social media posts not just in Pakistan but also in Europe and the USA. It represents an unprecedented attempt to enforce the jurisdiction of Pakistan's sharia courts extra-territorially.

Although there have been previous attempts to introduce a global Islamic blasphemy law, the Pakistani government has made more progress, for example meeting with a senior representative of FaceBook in July 2017 to discuss implementation.

Facebook, Twitter, YouTube and Microsoft also signed up to the European Commission Code of Conduct on Illegal Hate Speech in 2016. These regulations are intended to prevent racism and xenophobia and public incitement to violence or hatred directed against a group of persons or a member of such a group defined by reference to race, colour, religion, descent or national or ethnic origin, while maintaining freedom of expression, as defined by the European Court of Human Rights.

CHRISTIANS BRANDED AS TERRORISTS

In response to the horrific attack by an Islamic terrorist on a gay nightclub in Orlando, Florida, on 12 June 2016, which killed 49 people, President Obama stated that radical extremist groups view tolerance, diversity and women being empowered as a threat. He added, 'And unfortunately, that's something that the LGBT community is subject to not just by ISIL [the Islamic state group], but by a lot of groups that purport to speak on behalf of God around the world.' (Saine, 2016) In so doing, Obama subtly linked terrorists with Christians who do not endorse homosexual behaviour.

Even more troubling was the comparison of evangelicals to the terrorist group Al Qaeda. drawn by Nicholas Powers, American author and English professor. In his 2015 article 'The "War on Terror" and Gay Marriage: How a Generation Turned Against Religious Extremism' he wrote:

> A sweeping change has transformed our nation [the USA]. Surprisingly, during the "war on terror," the LGBT community has gone from social pariah to a symbol of global progress. Millennials especially support gay rights. An unseen feedback loop has propelled them into a progressivism: The more evangelicals demanded holy law in public spaces, the more they reflected Al Qaeda. In the eyes of many US youth, the face of the Muslim extremists routinely demonized by political leaders and the Christian extremists in their own back yards overlapped into one.

TRENDS USED TO MARGINALISE AND VILIFY CHRISTIANS IN THE WEST

Attacks on Christians have become so frequent, that it is now possible to identify consistent trends in the hostilities.

Use of government resources
Secular humanist and minority rights groups working within legal frameworks use the state to bring legal charges against Christians. Worryingly, these cases are criminal rather than civil. Churches and Christians have to fund their own legal costs while the 'aggrieved' party has almost unlimited resources available as the state prosecutes on their behalf. Once the case is won in a criminal court, the Christian or Christian organisation can be sued for damages in a civil court.

Forced entrapment
This is used by LGBT activists and groups to trap Christian individuals, churches and businesses.

- Groups opposed to Christianity scrutinize church websites, social media and publications, particularly statements of faith, employment criteria, membership criteria, doctrinal statements, and training or discipleship material.

- LGBT activists attend church services or listen to podcasts of sermons to see if they can find evidence of discrimination.

- LGBT individuals apply for positions to churches or Christian businesses and accuse the employer of discrimination if their application is rejected.

- Christians are asked to comment on controversial issues and then attacked for their Biblical views.

- LGBT customers demand Christian businesses to deliver services that are in blatant conflict with Biblical teaching — for example, Christian bakers or florists have been asked to serve same-sex marriages, as we have seen above.

- People in work places approach Christians with problems and the Christian offers to pray for them or shares their faith. The person who approached the Christian makes a complaint to the authorities. A number of Christian nurses and teachers have been targeted in this manner.

Trolling and Vilification by Popular Opinion

Social media or the mainstream media are used to vilify Christians. Anonymous individuals, referred to as 'trolls' in internet slang, stalk Christians on social media, chatrooms and blogs. Trolls instigate disputes and provoke an inflammatory discussion, often accompanied by offensive and threatening messages. The aim is to provoke readers into an emotional response or otherwise disrupt purposeful discussion on a particular topic. Other trolls then join the abuse by continuing to ridicule or threaten the victim. If the content is reposted, the issue can quickly go viral, that is, spread quickly on the internet, even globally. Trolls hunt for and join in Christian discussions or try to entrap Christians who have voiced an opinion contrary to prevailing opinions; these Christians may suddenly find themselves at the centre of widespread abuse. Sometimes there are threats of sexual or physical abuse and even death threats.

CONCLUSION

Freedom of speech and freedom of religion have been the bedrock of Western democracy. These twin pillars of freedom are now under the most severe attack imaginable, as Christians are accused, convicted and condemned by law for simply holding and expressing views that have been mainstream in Western society centuries. It is beyond doubt that the radical restructuring of the legal framework in Western countries is leading to the criminalisation of traditional Christian beliefs and practices. Instead of standing resolutely against this onslaught, the Church has largely capitulated to the new Babylonian captivity of Western society. It has lost the most essential core of its being — its identity. We will explore the problem of Christian identity in the next chapter.

8
CHRISTIAN IDENTITY — THE HEART OF THE PROBLEM

Behind the political and social crisis of the church in modern society, there stands the Christological crisis: From whom does the church really take its bearings? Who is Jesus Christ, really, for us today? In this identity-crisis of Christianity, the question of God lies hidden: Which God governs Christian existence — the one who was crucified or the idols of religion, class, race and society? Without a new clarity in Christian faith itself, there will be no credibility in Christian life. — Jürgen Moltmann (1973)

Identity is a complicated concept. Simply put, it is how a person or group sees themselves, and their place and purpose in the world. It is influenced by beliefs, culture, experiences, and the legacy of family, tribe, ethnic group or nation. When we speak of identity crisis we are implying that individuals or groups are confused about what they believe and what their purpose and place in the world is. In essence, their very being is in turmoil. The German theologian Jürgen Moltmann, writing his classic work *The Crucified God* in 1973, had already diagnosed an identity crisis facing Western Christianity and the Western Church. This crisis has intensified over the years, as we have seen in the preceding chapters. The Church desperately needs to clear this confusion and rediscover her true identity, her place in the world and the reason why she exists in the first place. Her survival in the West depends on this.

THE CHURCH IN NAZI GERMANY

Writing from a Nazi prison in 1944, the Lutheran pastor and theologian Dietrich Bonhoeffer reflected on how a seemingly Christian Europe could be plunged into a horrific war of global proportions. To its lasting shame, the Church was active in Germany, yet large sections of it ignored the actions of Hitler and the Nazi Party. Churches continued functioning as if everything was normal. They rationalised this divorce from reality by believing that the spiritual and physical worlds could operate separately without any apparent conflict or contradiction. Pastors preached sermons and congregations sang hymns with little or no comment or opposition to the totalitarian ideologies and unspeakable atrocities that marched across Europe. Indeed many Germans would have proudly called themselves Christian and Nazi without sensing any moral or spiritual dissonance. Bonhoeffer was one of the lone prophetic voices who challenged the Church and Christians for losing their true and primary identity.

> During the last year or so I've come to know and understand more and more the profound this-worldliness of Christianity. The Christian is not a *homo religiosus*, but simply a man, as Jesus was a man.... I'm still discovering right up to this moment, that it is only by living completely in this world that one learns to have faith. One must completely abandon any attempt to make something of oneself, whether it be a saint, or a converted sinner, or a churchman (a so-called priestly type!), a righteous man or an unrighteous one, a sick man or a healthy one. By this-worldliness I mean living unreservedly in life's duties, problems, successes and failures, experiences and perplexities. In so doing we throw ourselves completely into

the arms of God, taking seriously, not our own sufferings, but those of God in the world watching with Christ in Gethsemane. That, I think, is faith; that is metanoia; and that is how one becomes a man and a Christian.

In 1934, Bonhoeffer, Karl Barth and a few leading Christians issued the Barmen Declaration. This was a rebuke, warning, and appeal for repentance to the German Church as Hitler's ideology and ambitions became apparent. The Church was endorsing the emerging ideology by its silence and inaction. The Barmen Declaration affirmed the Lordship of Jesus Christ, His Word and Spirit over the church and the world, including all powers, principalities and cultures. It urged the church to examine herself, reform herself, seek her true identity, reclaim her morality, stand against injustices and rid herself of all influences that were contrary to the Gospel. The Barmen Declaration famously called upon the German Church to be a 'Confessing Church' — a church rejecting false doctrine as well as proclaiming and living by the truth. The German Church did not heed this warning. In 1939, Hitler plunged the world into a war costing the lives of tens of millions. Only after the war ended, a shocked and repentant Church began to reform herself.

LUTHER AND THE REFORMATION

Not just in Bonhoeffer's day, but all thorough history, the Church has from time to time strayed from her identity only to be led again into repentance and reformation. The Reformation (1517-1648) against the all-powerful might of the Roman Catholic Church is the classic case of a struggle for reform, renewal and regaining of the Church's identity, purpose and reason for existence. The Church in Europe and many other parts of the world was essentially the government of the day. Church and state were indistinguishable in that era of Christendom. Corruption, power and greed had corroded the medieval Church. She demanded uncritical obedience and misappropriated for herself the right to be the sole mediator between God and humanity. She even marketed the forgiveness of sins and entry to heaven in the form of 'indulgences.' In 1517, a rather unknown German monk, Martin

Luther, wrote his 95 Theses and nailed them to the door of a church in Wittenberg, triggering a confrontation of cataclysmic proportions with the all-powerful Roman Catholic Church. Luther's proposal was simple — the Bible alone is authoritative and salvation is by grace alone through faith alone. These ideas had been fermenting within some Christian circles but Luther was the catalyst for the great Reformation.

WESLEY AND THE REFORMATION IN BRITAIN

The Reformation swept across Europe. It gave birth to the Protestant movement. It compelled the Catholic Church to examine and reform herself. It prompted the Church in England to return to the authority of the Word of God. Francis White (1564-1638), an English reformer and contemporary of the Protestant Reformers, wrote:

> The Holy Scripture is the fountain and lively spring, containing in all sufficiency and abundance the pure Water of Life, and whatever is necessary to make God's people wise unto salvation ... The voice and testimony of the Primitive Church, is a ministerial and subordinate rule and guide, to preserve and direct us in the right understanding of the Scriptures.

Yet by the beginning of the 18th century, British Christianity had lost its identity. The Church of England had become a powerful governmental and political institution, serving the wealthy, educated, upper classes. Meanwhile, the poor and vulnerable were exploited, working conditions were dire, child labour was widespread, prostitution, thieving, gambling and sexual immorality were common place, and the slave trade was booming, but the Church of England did little to address the moral and social problems facing Britain. Sir William Blackstone (1723-1780) after visiting all the major churches in London commented that he 'did not hear a single discourse which had more Christianity in it than the writings of Cicero.' The philosopher and bishop George Berkeley (1685-1753) wrote that morality and religion in Britain had collapsed 'to a degree that was never known in any Christian country.'

An indelible stain on the Church's establishment is the story of the Codrington Plantation slaves. Christopher Codrington III was a wealthy sugarcane farmer in Barbados. He died in 1710 and bequeathed some of his lands and over 300 slaves to the Society for the Propagation of the Gospel in Foreign Parts (SPG), a missionary arm of the Church of England. (SPG was later renamed United Society of the Propagation of the Gospel (USPG), then United Society and in 2016 again changed its name to United Society Partners in the Gospel.) Not only did the SPG continue to keep the slaves, but it branded them with hot irons on their chests with the word 'Society' or the initials 'SPG.' The SPG purchased even more slaves and treated them harshly. Four out of every ten SPG slaves died within three years, many from ill treatment, disease and suicide. The SPG did not relinquish slave ownership until after the passing of Britain's Slavery Abolition Act in 1833.

It was at this time that John Wesley (1703-1791) began a movement of reform and revival in Britain. In the Church of England, Wesley's mother church, Christianity had become a matter of culture and national identity. Wesley understood that a faith that has no impact on how people live their everyday lives is not true Christianity. He wrote:

> I continue to dream and pray about a revival of holiness in our day that moves forth in mission and creates authentic community in which each person can be unleashed through the empowerment of the Spirit to fulfil God's creational intentions.

Wesley's views were not welcomed by the compromised and elitist Church of England and so he preached to the poor in prisons, hospitals, workhouses and mines, mostly in open air meetings. In his years of ministry he walked or travelled by horse over 400,000 kilometres across Britain and preached over 40,000 sermons. His tireless work led to the establishment of the Methodist denomination, charitable organisations, relief agencies, prison ministries, orphanages, schools, hospitals, mission agencies, the British and Foreign Bible Society, groups campaigning for the rights of women and children, and the beginnings of the anti-slavery movement. A great spiritual and social revival occurred within the church, which in turn affected all aspects of society. England was transformed and church and Christian identity re-established.

'Wesley practically changed the outlook and even the character of the English nation,' wrote Archbishop Davidson. Many historians credit Wesley and Whitfield with saving Britain from the bloody revolution movement that was sweeping across Europe at the time. As the nation turned to help the poor, repented of their sin, turned their hearts towards God and each other, a national transformation was taking place without the need for violence or revolution.

From his deathbed, Wesley wrote his last letter to William Wilberforce, Member of Parliament and a passionate evangelical Christian. Wesley had spoken out against slavery, calling it the 'execrable sum of all villainies.'

> But if God be for you, who can be against you? Are all of them stronger than God? O be not weary of well-doing! Go on, in the name of God and in the power of His might, till even American slavery (the vilest that ever saw the sun) shall vanish away before it.

Wilberforce rose to reform Church and country. On 28 October 1787, he wrote in his diary, 'God Almighty has set before me two great objects, the suppression of the Slave Trade and the Reformation of Morals.' Wilberforce's tireless efforts led first to the abolition of the slave trade and then to the abolition of slavery — for the first time in human history.

THE CHURCH AGAIN LOSES HER IDENTITY

Today's Western Church is once again trapped in a crisis of identity. She refuses to resist the dominant culture as in Nazi Germany. She submits to a corrupt form of Christianity as in the day of Luther and Wesley. Once upon a time bowing to the towering might of Christendom, today she unquestioningly surrenders to Western culture and swims with the tide of relativism and materialism in a post-Christian age. Western culture is now so deeply entrenched within the Church that it is difficult to distinguish between the two. The consequences of this can be seen in the moral decay of society. The Church is no longer the moral and spiritual voice of society and the moulder of a godly culture. Instead, she is the willing victim of an onslaught of ungodly liberalism. As we have seen in earlier chapters, there is little difference between Christian behaviour and that of Western society in general.

A vacuum of identity

The Church has abdicated her role within society. This, together with the alienation caused by an individualistic culture, has left an identity vacuum at the very heart of the West. In his book *On the Human Condition*, the French philosopher Dominique Janicaud has argued that in the absence of traditional religious definitions of our humanity and with increasing bio-technical advances in human engineering, Western culture is currently marked by an 'unprecedented uncertainty about human identity'.

Douglas Murray addressed this issue head-on in his book *The Strange Death of Europe: Immigration, Identity, Islam* (2017). Notice that he places the word 'identity' at the centre of the book's subtitle, flanked on either side by the twin forces of 'immigration' and 'Islam.' Murray underlines the crisis of identity:

> 'What am I doing here? What is my life for? Does it have any purpose beyond itself?' These are questions that have always driven human beings, questions that we have always asked and ask still. Yet for Western Europeans the answers to these questions that we have held onto for centuries seem to have run out. Happy as we are to acknowledge that, we are far less happy to acknowledge that with our story of ourselves having run out we are nevertheless still left with the same questions.

Murray, who is an atheist, happily accepts the role of Christianity and the Church in shaping Western civilisation and giving it its unique identity. He laments the death of Christianity in the West and the swelling tide of Islam rising to fill this vacuum.

> For some years now I have been especially struck by numerous accounts I have heard first hand and also read from people who have chosen to convert to Islam....The fact that they chose Islam is a story in itself. Why do these young men and women (very often women) not reach out and find Christianity? Partly it is because most branches of European Christianity have lost the confidence to proselytise or even believe in their own message. For the Church of Sweden, the Church of England, the German Lutheran Church and many other branches of European Christianity, the message of the religion has become a form of left-wing politics, diversity action and social welfare projects. Such churches argue for 'open borders' yet are circumspect about quoting the texts they once preached as revealed.

Murray correctly identifies the identity crisis within the Church. When she compromises her own historical beliefs and values, when she is perceived to be unreliable and uncertain in her convictions and mission, the Church offers little relief to a confused, corrupt yet desperate, identity-seeking West.

The vacuum of the Church's identity has become so pronounced that it recently prompted Humanist Lens, a humanist think tank, to comment on its effect on society in an article entitled 'Western Culture after Christendom.'

> This identity crisis extends from the most basic sense of who we are as human beings to the purpose of our cultural institutions, from a definition of humanity as such to the social values that our schools and courts are to implement. Honesty requires us to admit that our unmooring from religious sources of human dignity is largely to blame for this problem and that science, for all its innovative genius, is of little help in addressing it.

The Humanist Lens reluctantly concludes that the solution to the crisis is the 'retrieving the religious roots of humanism for contemporary society' (Zimmermann, 2011).

While many seek identity within Western ideologies and sub-cultures, in love from their families and friends and in leisure and pleasure, Rabbi Lord Jonathan Sacks warns of one consequence of the thirst for identity and the quest for an unwavering cause, belief and belonging in the absence of Judeo-Christian culture. Belonging and purpose have to be found elsewhere. He writes:

> In the West, the old marriage of religion and culture has ended in divorce. Our societies offer no clear values that appeal to young people looking for meaning, so religiously minded youths turn to the world beyond our borders where religion remains such a compelling force.

According to Lord Sacks, it is very often radical Islam that offers 'the sharpest, clearest voices they are hearing.'

THE CLARITY OF IDENTITY WITHIN ISLAM

Islam offers an attractive option for many people seeking purpose and meaning in life. Islam is based on three main elements — all profoundly integral to the concept of identity — belief, belonging, and behaviour.

- **Belief** is defined in the Islamic declaration of faith, the *shahada*. It has two parts: *la ilaha illa'llah* (there is no god but God), and *Muhammadun rasul Allah* (Muhammad is the messenger of God). This is the cornerstone of Islam. Once a person utters this creed, they are considered to be a Muslim. Devout Muslims recite the *shahada* 17 times a day during their five daily prayers. This creed affirms a person's identity within Islam. With other daily prayers and declarations, it provides an introduction to the faith, its expansionist mission in the form of *dawa* (mission) and jihad and its absolute beliefs. All these provide a well-defined sense of a purpose beyond the self-focussed consumerism of Western culture.

- **Belonging** comes by participation in the *umma*, the community of all Muslims worldwide, the nation of Islam. The *umma* is all-embracing and all-encompassing, caring for the needs of all its members. Apart from comfort, support, and security, the *umma* offers a radical alternative to the alienation of Western individualism and the breakdown of the nuclear family. The local mosque is central to the *umma*. Community springs forth from the mosque and the mosque shapes community and holds it together. The *umma* is such a strong bond that leaving Islam is regarded as treason and apostates from Islam face the death penalty, according to Islamic law.

- **Behaviour** is prescribed by Islamic law (sharia). Every part of a Muslim's life comes under the rule of sharia — diet, marriage, treatment of women, dress, education, finance, war and worship. Society can easily identify sharia-observant Muslims because of how they dress — beards, skullcaps and robes for men, hijabs covering the neck and hair of women, or more complete covering. Muslims can also be identified by the rituals and traditions they follow like prayer, almsgiving, fasting, and pilgrimage to Mecca. Islam even has a distinct greeting: *As-Salam-u-Alaikum wa-rahmatullahi wa-barakatuh* (Peace be unto you and so may the mercy of Allah and his blessings). This is followed by the reply *wa Alaikum Assalam wa Rahmatullah*. Many distinctive Muslim behaviours come from copying the model of Muhammad, as described in the *hadith* (traditions recording the words and actions of Muhammad and his early followers) which are considered almost as sacred as the Quran. It is from the *hadith* that Muslims learn they must not greet non-Muslims using the above Islamic greeting. 'Do not initiate the greeting of salaam to a Jew or a Christian'. These act as distinct identity markers which strengthen the sense of individual and communal identity, purpose, direction, and belonging to Islam.

With such clarity in defining identity and thoroughness in establishing identity, it is little wonder that Islam is the fastest growing religion in the world (especially in the West), and why the Church, flailing its arms in the midst of an identity crisis, is struggling to survive in the West.

The core components of Islamic identity also apply to Christian identity. Christians have used the traditional language of creed, community and commandments to frame the identity-markers of belief, belonging, and behaviour. For the Church and Christians to regain their identity, they must re-establish each of these as integral parts of their Christian faith and practice. We will examine these three elements in more detail in the next chapter.

9
CHRISTIAN IDENTITY — A WAY FORWARD

CREEDS

Knowing what to believe

The first stage of re-establishing Christian identity is knowing what to believe. The Western Church has been swamped by a sea of postmodern, relativist and humanist thinking, which has led to her confusion and crisis of identity. A 2008 Pew study of Christian beliefs in the United States revealed some startling facts. Only 72% of Protestants and 60% of Catholics believe that God is a personal being, meaning that He has the kind of properties that characterise a person (thoughts, values, emotions, etc.). The remainder view God as an impersonal force (like the Star Wars force or even gravity). Twenty percent of Christians do not believe in life after death. Sixty-six percent of Protestants and 79% of Catholics believe that other religions can lead to eternal life. Only 23% of Catholics and 46% of Protestants in the US believe that the Bible is the Word of God. These figures show just how unsure American Christians are about the most elementary doctrines of their faith.

In addition, twisted and distorted theologies are emerging within unbiblical church movements. Some offer 'custom-made designer Christianity' tailored to fit consumerist or postmodern worldviews. Hyper-grace, which emphasizes grace to the exclusion of repentance and confession of sin; universalist theology, which claims that everyone will be saved even without Christ; and gay theology, which affirms homosexuality as a gift from God, are three such examples. Dr Simon Chan, Professor of Systematic Theology at Trinity Theological College, Singapore, comments on a Church that has strayed from the core beliefs of Christianity.

> We end up not with the gospel of Jesus Christ but with propaganda, therapy, motivational talk, the gospel of health-and-wealth. Such "gospels" do not form a truly Christian identity, but create a deep identity crisis where Christians are no longer sure who they really are, and so end up being defined by the culture of this world. (2010)

At the end of the day, it is imperative for the Church to return to orthodoxy. This is not to be confused with the Orthodox Church (although there is much to learn from this form of Eastern Christianity). Orthodoxy is a Greek word meaning 'right worship' or 'right belief.' The Church must be certain of what it believes and its beliefs must be right. Roger Olson captures it succinctly:

> Orthodoxy is really — in the broadest and most generous sense — "mere Christianity." It is that core of essential beliefs denial of which results in serious distortion of the Christian message of the gospel and the Christian mission such that Christians become unrecognisable.

Statement of core beliefs
A creed is a Christian statement of core belief. The word creed comes from the Latin word 'credo,' which means 'I believe.' Creeds affirm the things that distinguish the Christian faith from the world's beliefs. Creeds also contain what Christians consider to be the absolute and non-negotiable truths of the faith. The early Church formulated

the most basic creeds in the writings of the New Testament. Biblical scholars agree that the shortest and earliest creed is the confessional statement of faith that 'Jesus is Lord.' Inspired by the Holy Spirit, the Biblical writers expanded this core into longer creeds in Philippians 2:6-11 and 1 Timothy 3:16. After the period of the apostles, the Church expanded on these creeds even further, as it sought to summarise the fundamental beliefs of Christian faith and simultaneously combat heresies that were creeping into the church. The best known are the Apostles' Creed and the Nicene Creed.

Professor Chan describes the importance of the creeds and orthodoxy, right worship and right belief, to Christian identity.

> One will not fail to notice, when attending a "liturgical" service, that there are many "speech-acts": The recitation of the Apostles' or Nicene Creed, the Lord's Prayer, various Trinitarian formulas (Holy, Holy, Holy; the Benediction), etc. This brings us to a central practice of Christian identity formation: It is primarily at worship that the basic Christian identity is shaped. When we worship the Father, through his Son and in the power of the Spirit, Christians are affirming who they really are: They are marked out as a people who worship the triune God who reveals himself in the redemptive work of Christ through the working of the Spirit.

The Church has strayed from these beliefs at various times throughout history. Luther's 95 Theses and Barth and Bonhoeffer's Barmen Declaration were in essence creedal statements, composed to re-establish the fundamentals of the Christian faith that had been eroded by the dominant cultures of the day. Creeds affirm, and when the Church has lost her identity, re-affirm the Lordship of Christ over everything — over culture, powers and authorities. There is no other alternative but for today's Church to return to the basics of the Christian faith. This creedal formation of Christian identity must happen corporately and individually — as the Church meets for worship and as individual followers of Jesus come before the throne of God in prayer.

Creeds must be integral to our lives

At the start of each school day, most American children pledge allegiance to the American flag. This is not an empty ritual or tradition. Instead, the practice is an identity former. It instils Americanism in the children, reminding them who they are and what they believe and stand for as a nation. This short, repetitive act creates a lifelong sense of identity based on nationality. Similarly, as we saw in the previous chapter, devout Muslims affirm their faith at least 17 times a day. However, within Christianity, churches are paying less and less attention to creeds, particularly in church services. Christians may go weeks, months or even years without a formal declaration of the fundamentals of their faith.

Non-conformist churches are reluctant to recite creeds during corporate worship because they want their worship to be spontaneous. Liberal churches avoid traditional creeds and compose contemporary statements of faith to incorporate the latest theological fad. Some churches simply do not wish to cause offence by expressing absolute truths in a postmodern culture. In an age of feel-good worship, where the self is the centre and therapy is the goal, worship-leaders may subconsciously decide not to use creeds because they exalt Christ rather than self as the focus of all worship. This strange creedal silence means that Christians are often unaware of the fundamentals of the faith and are defenceless against the influences of the many ungodly beliefs, voices and cultural norms. A study in 2004 revealed that half of Christians in the U.S. did not even know the meaning of 'grace.' 'Now that is pretty basic doctrine. Pastors today assume that their people know the basics. They don't,' remarks a Gallup study.

It goes without saying that the recitation of creeds must lead to a genuine heart experience of God or else it will be abstract and ineffective knowledge. At the same time, a living relationship with God needs a creedal scaffolding to protect it and hold it together against melting into a mushy Moralistic Therapeutic Deism. Tim Keller elaborates:

We must be able to existentially access our doctrinal convictions. If doctrinal soundness is not accompanied by heart experience, it will eventually lead to nominal Christianity — that is, in name only — and eventually to non-belief. The irony is that many conservative Christians, most concerned about conserving true and sound doctrine, neglect the importance of prayer and make no effort to experience God, and this can lead to the eventual loss of sound doctrine... Christianity without real experience of God will eventually be no Christianity at all. (2014)

There is an urgent need for churches to reinstate creedal statements as an integral part of both corporate worship and private worship. Congregations must regularly recite them and preachers must expound the doctrinal content of the ancient creeds — both to mature Christians and to new converts. In the murkiness of the battle that the Church and Christians are facing in the West, these declarations of belief and doctrine will act as banners demonstrating to ourselves and to the world who we are and what we stand for.

COMMUNITY

We desire to be in community

Belief has to go hand in hand with belonging; creeds must go together with full participation in community. Believing without belonging is meaningless and essentially contrary to the teaching of the Bible. Creed without community empties the creed of its content. The Christian faith is, at its very heart, about a relationship with God and our brothers and sisters in Christ.

Creeds and sound doctrine flow into a second stage of establishing identity: this is community or belonging to a group where others share the same beliefs. Community is practically non-existent in a Western culture defined by individualism and ravaged by family break-up. There is, therefore, a desperate longing to belong. The need to belong is a deeply embedded in human beings. Bilezikian puts it well in *Community 101: Reclaiming the Local Church as Community of Oneness*:

The silent churning at the core of our beings is the tormenting need to know and to be known, to understand and to be understood, to possess and to be possessed, to belong unconditionally and forever without fear of loss, betrayal, or rejection. It is the nostalgia for our primal oneness, the silent sorrowing for a paradise lost, the age-long pursuit after the encompassing embrace for which we know we were created. It is the search, however, wanton and sullied, for the pristine grace of holding and being held, for the freedom to be who we really are without shame or pretence, for release and repose in the womb-like safety of unalterable acceptance and of overarching love. (1997)

The Triune God has created us as social beings in His likeness: three persons in communion in one. In the Garden of Eden, God made space within His community for humankind. We lived in full community with God and with each other (Genesis 1:26-27, 2:18). However, with human rebellion, our relationship with a holy God was ruptured and consequently our relationship with one another has come apart. It is community that was the first casualty of the Fall. Animosity developed between man and woman and later between brothers — Cain and Abel. A primary aspect of discovering who we are as human beings and fulfilling that deep desire to belong is to re-establish our community with God. When we accept the authority of Jesus Christ as Lord and Saviour over our lives, we are re-connected with God. It is in our relationship and belonging to Christ that we find our true identity and are made complete. 'So you also are complete through your union with Christ, who is the head over every ruler and authority,' writes Paul (Colossians 2:10 New Living Translation).

Community with God requires time and effort
Although acceptance of Christ in our lives is vital to our salvation, many Christians are all too easily influenced by the world and feel distant from God. Any relationship is intentional — it takes time, effort, and communication. This applies to our relationship with God. The more time we spend in the Word and in prayer the closer our relationship is with the

Lord. Tim Keller in his book *Prayer: Experiencing Awe and Intimacy with God* points to prayer as a key component of realising our identity.

> To pray in Jesus' name [is], essentially, to reground our relationship with God in the saving work of Jesus over and over again. It also means to recognize your status as a child of God, regardless of your inner state.

Part of a family

Through our community with God, we are, by default, unavoidably made part of the wider community of the church. By virtue of belonging to Christ, we belong to His family, the Body of Christ. We simply cannot be part of the head (Christ), if we are not part of His body, the Church.

Our vertical relationship with God is incomplete and deficient without our horizontal relationship with other people who also share the same vertical relationship with God. If God is our Father, He does not leave us as lone children without brothers and sisters. He immediately places us into a wider family of fellow believers and children of God. Baptism is the enactment of this doctrine — we are incorporated into Christ's death and resurrection but we are also incorporated into the family of the Church. This belonging and identity extends to all believers past, present and future, into eternity. The word 'church' is derived from the Greek *kyriake* meaning 'belonging to the Lord.' Another Greek word for church is *ekklesia* or 'assembly.' The Church is an assembly of people who find their identity in their belonging to God. Professor Howard Macy of George Fox University puts it this way:

> Christian community is simply sharing a common life in Christ. It moves us beyond the self-interested isolation of private lives and beyond the superficial social contacts that pass for "Christian fellowship." The biblical ideal of community challenges us instead to commit ourselves to life together as the people of God.

Community or *koinonia* occurs 20 times in the New Testament. There is no English word that fully encapsulates the deep meaning of the

Biblical use of the Greek word *koinonia*. It encompasses communion, fellowship, participation, and being one part of a larger group. In essence, it is how God intends Christians to live together in fellowship and unity. *Koinonia* is a fundamental aspect of Christian identity. Theologians Karl Rahner and Harald Wagner emphatically link our relationship to God with our relationship to our fellow-believers:

> Salvation implies above all communion, *koinonia* among those to whom the conviction that Jesus Christ is the Saviour of the world was given in the first place. Just as it is impossible to belong to the *koinonia* without sharing in this conviction, it is fundamentally out of the question to believe in Christ without being incorporated into the hosts of those who share that belief. To maintain that it is legitimate and theologically acceptable to be a Christian without any relationship to the church is equal to a fatal rejection of the social, indeed incarnational, dimension of faith, and thus to an invalidation of faith itself. (Cited in Fuchs, 2008)

In other words, salvation allows us to enter the family of God, but, unless we have a relationship with the others in this family, our Christian faith is null and void.

What we can learn from the Church in the book of Acts

The word *koinonia* first appears in the Bible in Acts 2:42-47 — the passage serves as a model of community for today's Church.

> They devoted themselves to the apostles' teaching and to fellowship [*koinonia*], to the breaking of bread and to prayer. Everyone was filled with awe at the many wonders and signs performed by the apostles. All the believers were together and had everything in common. They sold property and possessions to give to anyone who had need. Every day they continued to meet together in the temple courts. They broke bread in their homes and ate together with glad and sincere hearts, praising God and enjoying the favour of all the people. And the Lord added to their number daily those who were being saved.

There are many practical lessons today's Church can learn from this example of community.

1. We must be devoted to the teachings of the Christian faith. Fellowship and community are not just about meeting together socially. They must include learning, studying and meditation on the Word.

2. Community must be intentional. It needs work. Relationships take time and effort. The early Church 'devoted themselves' to fellowship. They made time for each other. This is something that will require sacrifice and dedication in today's busy, individualistic, and entertainment-focused society. Community is now almost counter-cultural. Western culture has created whole generations that are socially challenged and do not know how to interact with others. A survey by One Poll discovered that 65% of millennials avoid face-to-face conversations so much so that 80% would rather text or email than speak directly to someone. Breaking the effects of the conditioning of Western culture, technology addiction and the limitations of social media will take deliberate effort, time, patience, understanding and above all love.

3. The primary function of *koinonia* is bonding together in community with God. It is God, through His Spirit, who joins us as one body. Communal prayer and worship allow the Holy Spirit to move amongst us, strengthening our bond with Him and with each other. Prayer to and worship of a living and personal God who is in relationship with us is a profound and integral part of Christian community.

4. We must not ignore the symbols and traditions of our faith. When the early Church met, they broke bread together. Community must allow the telling of the Christian story through the Lord's Supper, baptism, hymns, the cross, and creeds. These act as reminders to the Church but also as a witness to the world. They are identity markers of our faith.

5. Other translations of Acts 2:44 say that the believers were of one accord. This means that they were of one mind. They worked to

ensure that there were no divisions between them and there was harmony in the group. They knew who they were individually and as a group. The Church today must be clear about who she is and what she stands for. The early Church was made up of many different sub-groups that may not have met together in such a radical manner before they became disciples of Jesus. Men and women, free and slave, different racial and ethnic groups and various social classes all came together, breaking down previous barriers. A community must be inclusive of all people whatever their background, age, gender or racial group.

6. A community meets the needs of its members. Members must be sensitive to the spiritual and physical needs of others.

7. Meeting together must be regular. The early Church met daily. It may not be practical for many Christians now to meet every day. However, meeting together for one or two hours during a church service once a week (or even less frequently as many studies show of church attendance today) while living separate lives through the rest of the week is not sufficient to establish and maintain community and relationships.

8. The early Christians met in the temple courts. The local church can and must act as the centre and focal point of community life.

9. It was this demonstration of a loving and godly community that was so attractive to others. If community could be lived out as God intended, the Church would not be in the identity crisis she is in today. Instead, she would be an attractive answer to the loneliness of the world. The Lord would surely add greatly to our numbers.

Community has many functions. It is where we find love, acceptance, healing and care. It is where we are able to grow, receive encouragement and learn without fear of rejection or shame. However, is not just about us and having our own needs met. It is about identifying and meeting the needs of others, by living in mutual submission and in service to each other. In an individualistic age plagued by superficial relationships, the Church must intentionally create space for community. This will not at first be comfortable or natural for many Christians who have been conditioned by Western culture to exist outside of a godly community. The enemy hates unity and will do all he can to sow discord and disharmony amongst the Body of Christ through frivolous offences, quarrels, splits and divisions but more subtly by simply drifting out of community. This is not a new battle. The writer to the Hebrews warns of it:

> And let us consider how we may spur one another on toward love and good deeds, not giving up meeting together, as some are in the habit of doing, but encouraging one another — and all the more as you see the Day approaching. (Hebrews 10:24-25)

Community is evangelistic

Jesus said, 'By this everyone will know that you are my disciples, if you love one another' (John 13:35). A vibrant, strong and committed community is inherently evangelistic. It is the embodiment of Christ on earth. It is an example to a watching and searching world of the ideal of the fullness of human existence, of love, forgiveness, acceptance and belonging. It is what the world consciously or unconsciously hungers for in the depths of its soul. This can only be achieved if the Church and believers are distinct from the corrupt worldly culture in which they exist. Why would the world want to belong to the Body of Christ if there were no difference between it and a social or sports club? The Christian community must demonstrate a clear sense of belief, identity and purpose.

Christian community must not be exclusive. It exists to expand and to invite others into it. It is here that one of the most important functions of community takes place, that of discipleship. Discipleship is the spiritual formation or creation of Christian identity. In other words, community is where believers are taught what it means to be a follower of Christ and a member of His family. It is not enough to attend church services. Christians, especially new Christians, need to be mentored, that is, guided by a wise counsellor. Just as a convert from Islam may take time to understand how Christianity differs from Islam, so too a convert from Western culture will have to go through a learning process to find out how Christianity differs from Western culture. There is a real and urgent need to disciple many long-standing members of the Church who remain greatly influenced by un-Christian elements of Western culture.

COMMANDMENTS

Our identity is demonstrated by our actions

In 2004, George Gallup, the founder of the Gallup survey group, addressed the Gordon Conwell Theological Seminary in Boston and reflected on his more than 50 years of polls and studies. His primary observation was that he could not understand how a nation where 86% of the population believed in God and about half claimed to attend church each week was also a society wracked by domestic problems of fatherlessness, abuse of children and women, crime, sexual promiscuity and immorality. He said:

> Surveys reveal an unprecedented desire for religious and spiritual growth among people in all walks of life and in every region of the nation. There is an intense searching for spiritual moorings, a hunger for God. It is for churches to seize the moment and to direct this often vague and free-floating spirituality into a solid and lived-out faith ... Someone has to challenge people to be true disciples of Christ. Someone has to ask the hard questions. If we don't talk about the whole dimension of sin, repentance, grace and forgiveness, what is the faith all about? What are we doing ... Without true discipleship, the church can simply turn into a social services agency.

A key component of identity is behaviour. We may believe certain things, we may be part of a community, but if our lives and behaviour do not reflect our beliefs and the fundamentals of Christianity, we are part of the Church's identity crisis. The apostle James reminds us that belief is not a sufficient requirement to be a Christian. He insists that a faith that has no deeds is no good (James 2:14-19). With scathing sarcasm, James points out that even demons believe in God! Our faith is demonstrated by our deeds. The Church is facing a crisis because it is indistinguishable from non-Christians. Just as God is holy (i.e. set apart) so too are we called to be set apart from the world (1 Peter 1:16). Jesus says that if we love Him we will obey His commandments (John 14:15) and 'You are my friends if you do what I command' (John 15:14). 'Whoever says, "I know him," but does not do what he commands is a liar, and the truth is not in that person,' writes John (1 John 2:4). In an uncertain world, we can be certain of our identity in Christ if we obey His commandments. John goes on to warn believers of the very real danger of being blinded and losing our way, if we reject community by hating our fellow-Christians and disobey God's commandments by living in habitual sin (1 John 1:9-11). Sin is a demonstration of an identity crisis and results in further distancing from God and therefore a deeper identity crisis. It is a vicious spiral. And so, to be part of the Church and to be certain of who we are, we must adhere to and delight in following the Lord's commandments.

Commandments tell us how to live well

Many of Jesus' commandments are about love. Jesus commands us to love God (Matthew 22:37), our neighbour (Matthew 22:39), one another (John 13:34), and our enemies (Matthew 5:44). In addition, the Bible repeatedly stresses correct living. Paul provides a useful study of how to live in Galatians 4 to 6. He tells us that we have been set free from blind obedience to the norms of the culture in which we live; on occasion Christian living may even bring us into conflict with the laws of the land. Paul reminds us that Christ has set us free from the bondage of the law but we must not use this freedom to live in sin. On the contrary, when we live by grace, we are called to a higher standard. Paul goes on to list sinful acts like sexual immorality, impurity, drunkenness, idolatry, witchcraft, hatred, disunity, jealousy, anger, and selfish ambition. Other parts of the Bible list sins such as lying, deceiving and spreading rumours to destroy others. Paul tells us that if we live by the Spirit we will produce spiritual fruit in our lives: love, joy, peace, patience, kindness, goodness, faithfulness, gentleness and self-control. He also mentions that we must do good to all people, especially other Christians.

Homosexual practice

What should the Christian attitude be to people following a homosexual lifestyle? How should we relate to them?

First, we must examine our own hearts and confess to God any prejudices that we find within ourselves.

Second, we should carefully consider our mental picture of these individuals: is it a fair picture? Have we recognised their good qualities? Many are particularly kind, gentle, considerate and thoughtful people.

Third, we should check that our posture towards them is one of respect and love. We are respectful, remembering that they are created by God in His image (*imago dei*), and we are loving, following the example of our Lord Jesus Christ who loved everyone.

When we have followed these three steps, we can then go on to the fourth step, which is to set out our position, in discussion with them. Our position will be founded on the Bible and its authority. We may quote the Bible, and we will rely on the authority of God's Word to respond to human arguments such as claims by medical science that homosexual desires are innate and therefore must be yielded to.

There is no better way to be clear about our identity — both to ourselves and to others — than to live a righteous and godly life. We must recognise within ourselves that we are influenced by the world and we must renew our hearts and minds continually. We must be clear about what is right and wrong and live without compromise in this postmodern age. We have an obligation to do this as individual Christians and as the Church. Only then can we influence society instead of allowing society to influence us.

Renewal of hearts, minds and actions

It is vital for us as individuals and the Church to undergo a radical transformation or *metanoia*. Bonhoeffer mentions *metanoia* in his letter from prison. *Metanoia* is a Greek word meaning a deep spiritual conversion. It is a change of heart and mind, of thoughts, actions and being. In other words, it is moving away from a misguided identity to one of true identity. Strong's commentary defines *metanoia* as

> a change of mind: as it appears in one who repents of a purpose he has formed or, of something he has done, especially the change of mind of those who have begun to abhor their errors and misdeeds, and have determined to enter upon a better course of life, so that it embraces both a recognition of sin and sorrow for it and hearty amendment, the tokens and effects of which are good deeds.

Another commandment, sometimes called the Great Commission, is outlined in Matthew 28:18-20. Here, Jesus speaks of the need to tell others about the Gospel and teach them how to follow Him. This means showing people how to live well under the authority of God. God has given us a set of guidelines in Scripture to live by for our own good and for the good of the world. If we live by these guidelines we will find a sense of internal and external peace and wholeness which the Bible calls *shalom*.

In a postmodern, relativist age with few absolutes, sin is hardly ever spoken of in church or when we share our faith with others. Nate Wilson, in his study *The Essentials of the Kerygma: What we must Preach,* observes that the Gospel is presented 18 times in the book of Acts and in every instance both sin and judgement are mentioned. Wilson writes:

> So whatever we do in our presentations of the Gospel, we must point out the fact that our audience has sinned and will be judged for it. It is interesting to note that the apostles are gentler with those more ignorant of sin and harsher with those who have more knowledge of God. In the two encounters with pagans who were utterly unexposed to the true God (Lystra and the Æropagus), God's grace is emphasized: 'In the past, he let all nations go their own way' (Acts 14:16); 'In the past God overlooked such ignorance...' (Acts 17:30). However, when speaking to people who should have known better

the apostles could be quite harsh: Peter yelled at Simon, a believer, "May your silver perish with you!" and Paul also had choice words for the High Priest, "God shall smite you, you whitewashed wall!" To whom much is given, much is required.

The Bible does not shy away from the need to be righteous and to repent of sin. Rather, this is the crux of the Gospel. If the Church is to be a witness in the world she can no longer fail to address the issue of sin in society and indeed within the Church herself, but she must do this in a loving and gentle yet resolute and firm manner.

Our responsibility

Some believe that the Great Commission is a call not only to reach out to individuals within the nations but also to the nations themselves. Throughout history, the Church moulded and shaped society. Sociologist Rodney Stark, in his book *The Rise of Christianity,* reviews the influence of the Church in one of the most immoral and godless periods: the period in which the Church was born.

> Christianity served as a revitalization movement that arose in response to the misery, chaos, fear, and brutality of life in the urban Greco-Roman world.... Christianity revitalized life in Greco-Roman cities by providing new norms and new kinds of social relationships able to cope with many urgent problems. To cities filled with the homeless and impoverished, Christianity offered charity as well as hope. To cities filled with newcomers and strangers, Christianity offered an immediate basis for attachment. To cities filled with orphans and widows, Christianity provided a new and expanded sense of family. To cities torn by violent ethnic strife, Christianity offered a new basis for social solidarity. And to cities faced with epidemics, fire, and earthquakes, Christianity offered effective nursing services.... For what they brought was not simply an urban movement, but a new culture capable of making life in Greco-Roman cities more tolerable.

This process was not without cost. The early Church went through the most extreme and horrific persecution. Multitudes were martyred under the Emperor Nero (54-68) and other Roman emperors like Domitian (81-96), Decius (249-251), Gallus (251-253), Valerian (257), Diocletian (284-305), Galerius (305-311) and Maximinus (311-312). A number of Roman emperors made Christianity subject to capital punishment. Christians could avoid death if they renounced their faith by offering a sacrifice to the Roman gods, or to Caesar who had come to be considered a god. But the early Christians were so sure of their identity in Christ that they refused to submit to any other god, even under the most excruciating torture and the most horrific deaths. Christians were stoned, thrown to the lions, burnt alive, boiled in oil, skinned alive and crucified upside down. Despite or because of this persecution the Church grew and thrived. Many Romans watching the public spectacle of Christians singing praises to God as they faced death without fear or hatred of their persecutors wondered at the certainty of their faith. 'Rome could cope with revolutions; she could not cope, as history demonstrated, with a community owing imitative allegiance to the crucified and risen Jesus,' writes historian and theologian N. T. Wright.

Christians and a Church with a crystal-clear and razor sharp identity can and must be an influence in the world again. The early Church and the reformations mentioned in Chapter 8 are from very different ages and contexts. Nevertheless, in each case faithful believers, facing seemingly insurmountable odds, were able to lead the wider Church to rediscover its identity through repentance and reform. This offers tremendous hope and encouragement to faithful believers of today. Given reflection, repentance and reformation, the wayward Church can rediscover its identity and once again reclaim its place as the shaper of morality and godly living in the West. The flickering flame can once again burst into a blazing fire. It is our joy, duty and responsibility to be part of this call to a new reformation.

10
CONCLUSION

I was visiting the magnificent Duomo — the Cathedral of Santa Maria del Fiore — in Florence on 1 August 2016. Access to the pews was roped off. There was nowhere to sit or pray. Another visitor, equally frustrated, said he was going to climb over the rope and sit in the front pew. I joined him and soon our wives came and sat with us — all of us fixing our eyes on a large carving of Jesus on the cross. The stranger struck up a conversation with me. He wondered why in the Cathedral of all places, there was nowhere to sit and pray, and wasn't sure if someone would come and move us from our chosen seats at the foot of the cross.

He also commented how horrified Jesus would be to see the opulence and ostentation of the building — a glaring contrast to His teaching and simple lifestyle. I asked him where he came from. He told me he was from Pakistan. 'Are you a Christian?' I enquired. 'No, a Muslim,' he replied. He was seeking truth, meaning, and simplicity, making forays into every religion he came across. But in post-Christian Europe he had found nothing to help him in various churches, only grandeur and outward pomp. I, myself, had searched in vain for a Bible in all the famous cathedrals of Italy which I had visited that summer.

The Italian cathedral where I had the conversation I have described above, is a stone's throw from the spot where Savonarola and two of his followers were hanged and burned on 23 May 1498. Girolamo Savonarola, an Italian Dominican friar and preacher, had condemned the wealth and excesses of his fellow clergy and called them to repentance. In response, the church's hierarchy 'crucified' their own in order to maintain their position, status and power. And so the Western Church continues, through history and today, paying lip service to the ideals of Christ and the Christian faith, but all too often turning into a self-serving Judas.

Sadhu Sundar Singh, an Indian convert from Sikhism who died in 1929, compared the church to a kind of boulder in the Himalayas which, when smashed open, reveal a hollow interior. The same geological marvel is found in New Zealand, where the smooth round boulders scattered across the beach near Moeraki are just empty shells of rock.

Too many churches in the West are now like these hollow boulders — imposing shells with little substance or strength inside. It is not only in the grand cathedrals of Italy where it is almost impossible to find a Bible. Try looking for a Bible or hymnbook in many evangelical churches in the UK, and you will be hard-pressed to find one. You will, undoubtedly, be told with a mildly condescending smile, that all the words the congregation needs are projected on a screen when the time comes to sing or read the Word of God. In many congregations, people now read the Bible from their smart phones, so paper books are redundant.

While this is all logical and economical and helps to keep the church sanctuary looking tidy, it does mean that visitors to church buildings find no spiritual help. Nor can worshippers waiting for a Sunday service to begin pick up a book and contemplate the words of a hymn or a Scripture passage to prepare their hearts and minds for the service.

There is a dearth of the Scriptures in our lands. Even if this is in part due to the advances of technology, is it also symptomatic of a lack of respect for God's Word? The prophet Amos foretold a 'famine of hearing the words of the Lord. Men will stagger from sea to sea and wander from north to east, searching for the word of the Lord, but they will not find it' (Amos 8:11-12). In places where Christians are actively persecuted, the persecutors will often strain every nerve to halt the publication of the Bible and Christian literature, because they know how important these resources are to strengthen the faith of Christians. They forbid printing, importing and selling any form of Christian literature, and police raids confiscate Christian books that have somehow found their way into the possession of believers. In the West, though, there are no such reasons for a lack of the Holy Scriptures. It is local churches who reduce the availability of the Word of God.

There is a well-known jibe about Christianity in Africa being 5,000 miles wide and an inch deep. But could not the same be said of North American Christianity? There is a great deal of churchgoing on Sundays, but, as we have seen in chapters three and four, little discernible difference between Christians and non-Christians during the rest of the week.

And what are the dimensions of European Christianity? Here it is not only the shallow depth that is a concern but also the rapidly diminishing width. The presence of the Christian faith in the public square has greatly declined, and churchgoing on Sundays (the most visible activity of a practising Christian) is seen as an abnormal and freakish habit — indeed, even practising Christians no longer consider it an obligation to keep the Lord's Day holy.

For those who do go to church, what difference does it make? Congregations attending liturgical worship come out of church on a Sunday outwardly praising the aesthetics of the service and inwardly reassured of their respectability. Charismatic Christians come out pumped-up by the emotional uplift of the exuberant worship they have participated in but unable to say what they have learned of God. In the reformed traditions, church members delight in the skilfully constructed sermons and go home saying they have been edified by the expository teaching, yet like the others they eat their Sunday lunch and continue with their lives unchanged.

A group of young people, describing themselves as passionately committed to Christ and studying at Cambridge, one of Britain's noblest universities, would attend Sunday worship dressed in jeans with designer holes in them. On Saturday nights they would get drunk. They could not reconcile the way they lived with what they believed.

The disconnected lives of the Cambridge students are typical of many Christians in the West. They drink of the cup of a secular materialist humanist society which shapes their minds and gives them the desires for hedonist pleasures which consume their existence. Yet, they claim to practise a Christian faith to varying degrees. So their lives are compartmentalised and not integrated. But as the poison in their cup begins to take effect, the balance shifts. Some turn into fake Christians, like the hollow boulders of the Himalayas and New Zealand, going through the motions of being a Christian but not realising there is no inner substance left. Others cast off the faith altogether.

It is easy to make this transition while remaining blissfully unaware that the Bible is full of warnings about it. Jeremiah spoke of those who had abandoned God, the source of living water, and dug cisterns for themselves that were cracked and could not hold water (Jeremiah 2:13). Jesus spoke of those who have ears but cannot hear, and eyes but do not see (Mark 8:18).

In the book of Revelation, the risen Christ delivers a prophecy to seven local churches in the land that was known as the province of Asia in the first century. Could it be that the three churches that share striking similarities with the Western Church today are the churches of Ephesus, Thyatira and Laodicea — as we shall see below?

APOSTASY

The early church used the term 'apostasy' to name and shame those who had abandoned Christianity for another religion. Apostasy can be a state of the heart or a state of the mind — or both.

The mind may continue to give assent to the central doctrines of the Christian faith. It may continue to own Christ as Lord. It may continue to engage in the act of worship. Yet if the heart is not centred on Christ, filled with Christ, if Christ does not own the heart, then the heart defects, departs or revolts — hurtling down the broad road into the barren land of apostasy.

The heart is the seat of our emotions, the cockpit of our lives. It is the basis of our desires. When our heart is centred on Christ, then He becomes the centre of our existence. Without Him we have no being, for in Him we live and move and have our being. He is our home here on earth, and when we have shed our earthly bodies, He will continue to be our home in glory.

Christians down the ages have faced the challenge of apostasy. Jesus warned, "Not everyone who says to me, 'Lord, Lord,' will enter the kingdom of heaven, but only the one who does the will of my Father who is in heaven. Many will say to me on that day, 'Lord, Lord, did we not prophesy in your name and in your name drive out demons and in your name perform many miracles?' Then I will tell them plainly, 'I never knew you. Away from me, you evildoers!'"(Matthew 7:21-23)

The Gospels tell the tragic tale of would-be followers of Jesus who turned back. Even among the inner circle of the Twelve, there was one — Judas — who betrayed Jesus. Jesus battled constantly for the hearts of his disciples. In denial, in failure, they gradually learned what it was for Him to possess their hearts.

Then they were set on fire. It was a fire that burned so brightly that nothing could dim the intensity of the light. It was a fire that rapidly spread throughout the known world. Through Christ, they had become more than conquerors (Romans 8:37).

Yet the flame soon began to dim, and before long was at risk of being extinguished in some places where it had once blazed brightly and warmly. Jesus rebuked the church in Ephesus, 'I hold this against you: You have forsaken the love you had at first. Consider how far you have fallen! Repent and do the things you did at first. If you do not repent, I will come to you and remove your lampstand from its place.' (Revelation 2:4-5) This was a church commendable for its sound doctrine, hard work and perseverance in the face of hardship. But even this was not enough if their love for Jesus had grown cold.

By contrast, the church in Thyatira, which like Ephesus was commended by the Lord for its service and perseverance, had much of love but little of the sound doctrine of the Ephesians. Jesus condemns the church of Thyatira for tolerating the teachings of a prophetess who misled its Christians into sexual immorality and eating food sacrificed to idols. It was an apostate church. (Revelation 2:19-20)

Jesus reserved his most excoriating words for the wishy-washy church in the prosperous city of Laodicea. 'I know your deeds, that you are neither cold nor hot. I wish you were either one or the other! So, because you are lukewarm — neither hot nor cold — I am about to spit you out of my mouth.' Their smug and ignorant apathy was as serious in Christ's eyes as the outright apostasy of Thyatira and they were about to be completely rejected by Him. (Revelation 3:15-16)

The Ephesians and the Laodiceans were teetering on the brink of apostasy, not because of persecution but because of self-love which led to indifference to Christ. The Thyatirans had gone a step further and had actually apostatised, learning 'Satan's so-called deep secrets,' yet they continued to consider themselves a church of Christ's disciples.

HAS THE CHURCH IN THE WEST TURNED APOSTATE?

This is not an easy question to answer. If the Church as a corporate body forsakes her Lord and embraces the world, then she has turned apostate. No matter how professional her organisational status, how grand her liturgy, how respectable her existence, if she embraces the God-denying laws of the land and the decadent culture and norms of non-believers, if she is guided by the secular principles and diktats of the nation in which she lives, then she is apostate — she has defected and has committed high treason against Christ — for He is no longer at the helm and centre, with His commands, His laws, His priorities, and His norms.

After the Church of England's General Synod passed its resolutions in favour of transgenderism and homosexuality in 2017, Biblical scholar and columnist Jules Gomes pointed out that, in the 500th year of the Reformation, the church had 'crossed the thin red line from apostolic to apostate.' The article entitled 'Apostate Church of England has mutated into a Gnostic "Sex" Sect,' cited Susie Leafe, Director of Reform, who explained how 'In the space of four days, the General Synod of the Church of England has, in effect, rejected the doctrines of creation, the fall, the incarnation, and our need for conversion and sanctification.'

Another characteristic of the contemporary Western Church is the more than comfortable lifestyles of so many of its leaders. Mega-churches, mission agencies and advocacy organisations pay their top executives way above average salaries. In this, they follow the scandalous behaviour of many secular charities. Exorbitant staff pay contributes to the disgracefully high overheads of many Christian charities, who seek support from ordinary Christians, many of them poor pensioners giving sacrificially from small incomes. These widows' mites are squandered by organisations which spend over 50% of their income in advertising, salaries and other internal costs.

Jesus warned that no one can serve both God and money. If you are devoted to one, you will hate and despise the other (Matthew 6:24). Distressingly, it seems that many in the Western church love and serve money. Justin Welby, Archbishop of Canterbury, dished out bonuses totalling £1,048,000 to ten of the Church of England's fund managers in 2016. This was paid on top of the fund managers' already very substantial salaries. The secular press attacked Welby for his hypocrisy, because when the Archbishop was on the Parliamentary Commission on Banking Standards he had accused banks of 'hypocrisy' for paying their staff huge bonuses.

Around the same time, a new Anglican province was being formed in Sudan, one of the world's poorest countries, with a strongly Islamic population, where Christians are severely persecuted. The new province could afford to pay its clergy only a pittance, leaving them to survive as best they could. The Church of England offered no financial assistance at all to the running costs of the courageous new province. The African Anglicans did not receive a penny from the overpaid and well-funded English Anglicans. Furthermore, hundreds of thousands of Christians, including many Anglicans, had fled from South Sudan to Uganda and were dying of starvation. There was evidently no feeling or concept of responsibility for fellow-Christians or a sense of being part of the one Body of Christ.

How will the Western church stand before the Lord Jesus on the Day of Judgement and what will it have to say for itself? Swayed by secularism, infected by postmodernism, riddled with materialism — can it build hollow cathedrals only in hay and straw — empty structures that will be burnt up by God's all-consuming fire? (1 Corinthians 3:12-15)

The cancer of apostasy not only eats away at structures but also devours Christians and churches. Jesus calls His followers to be pilgrims and strangers on earth, whose only real dwelling is the heavenly realm. Their hearts belong to God and their eyes gaze on the One they love. They own no other Lord or Master. They live for Him alone and for His glory alone. Once they deviate from the straight and narrow path of discipleship, the only broad way open to them is the highway of apostasy. This has been the challenge to Christians throughout the ages and is worked out daily in minor and major acts of living. The only oil that will keep the fire of faith ablaze is the oil of our first love for Jesus.

Perhaps God in His mercy will send a new Wesley or Whitfield, empowering them to spark off a new era of spiritual transformation, and revival and holiness will sweep like a forest fire across the nations of the West. Then, we will again see the Church rise like a phoenix from her heap of ashes leading to a cultural revolution as profound as that in eighteenth-century Britain, which many believe saved Britain from a bloody revolution such as France had endured.

REVIVAL AND REVERSAL

We must pray for a new revival that will impact first the Western church and then Western society. Such a revival will turn today's norms upside down. It will magnify the Lord, as Mary did in her song of praise (Luke 1:46). God has been diminished and made very small by secular humanist societies which magnify humankind. This must be reversed, with God praised, honoured and lifted high, while the overweening self-esteem of human beings is reduced to a Biblical humility and attitude of dependence on God's mercy.

God's holiness must be recognised (Luke 1:49). Biblical holiness must once more become the goal of believers. This reverses the present position where Christians follow society's erroneous lead on morality and ethics, with no sense of the awe, majesty and holiness of God.

The materialism and greed, which riddle both society and the Western church to the point where even the most committed Christians are all but blind to the grotesque paradox of their luxurious lifestyles, must be abandoned. Christians must learn, once again, to store up treasure in heaven, to use their money to help those in need, and to value simplicity (Luke 1:53). Maybe society will sicken of its excesses and follow suit.

Mary also sang of the Lord bringing down the powerful and lifting up the lowly (Luke 1:52). How desperately both society and church need this reversal — that the weak and lowly may no longer be trampled down and trodden underfoot.

Mary was supremely focused on Christ. Her song of praise poured out in response to the prophetic words of her cousin Elizabeth who, guided by the Holy Spirit, spoke of the baby in Mary's womb as the Lord. Mary's womb was filled with Jesus just as Mary's mind was filled with Holy Scripture. Mary's song, sometimes called the Magnificat, is a mosaic of 21 Old Testament references, including 16 references to the Psalms. Mary knew her Bible. Reversing the current famine of God's Word, the Church must focus once again on Christ and His Word — the Bible — remaining faithful to both.

Western society has undergone a massive cultural transformation, disastrously affecting the Western church. We must pray for a spiritual transformation of both church and society, claiming God's ancient promise to His people. 'If my people, who are called by my name, will humble themselves and pray and seek my face and turn from their wicked ways, then I will hear from heaven, and I will forgive their sin and will heal their land.' (2 Chronicles 7:14)

PREPARE FOR PERSECUTION

What if God does not bring the earthquake of reversal and the fire of revival? In that case, Christians in the West who are faithful in their love for the Lord must prepare for persecution. As anti-Christian pressures rise and lure Christians into apathy and apostasy, the faithful remnant will have to be ready to suffer or else to go into hiding as an underground church — and from there to mount a guerrilla resistance against the world and Satan's throne.

How should Christians prepare for this? Disciples of Jesus should study and learn from persecuted Christians past and present, so that when suffering comes they will stand firm, with their faith intact. They must fill their hearts and minds with the Scriptures (memorising as much as possible) to strengthen them when that suffering comes. They must familiarise themselves with the stories of the martyrs, how they built up their faith, and what they thought, prayed and said when under pressure to deny Christ. They will have to seek each other out, for denominational labels will be of little use in finding the faithful remnant, who are likely to be scattered within every Christian community. The remnant must start meeting together, tear away from pseudo-Christians, gathering perhaps in homes or other venues rather than church buildings, to encourage each other in a robust Biblical faith and a truly Christian culture that stands against the tide of society. They must be ready to help one another financially as some may lose their jobs or need to pay legal fees for their defence in court.

All through the pages of history, there has always been a remnant seeking to be faithful, like Savonarola. The Lord sees them, knows them and loves them. Jesus had a message for the faithful remnant at Thyatira — for those who rejected the false teaching of their leaders that other Thyatiran Christians had swallowed. It was their only comfort — but what a great comfort for those individuals to know that the King of kings and Lord of lords was aware of their struggles and distress. The message was simple and stark: 'Only hold on to what you have until I come.' (Revelation 2:24-25)

SOURCES AND REFERENCES

"10 Fundmentals of Religion in Sweden." *Sweden.se*, 2017, https://sweden.se/society/10-fundamentals-of-religion-in-sweden/ (accessed 24 August 2017).

Abbott, Douglas. "Do Lesbian Couples Make Better Parents than Heterosexual Couples?" *International Journal of Humanities and Social Science.* Vol. 2, No. 13 (2012) pp. 30-46.

Alleyne, Richard. "Lying children will grow up to be successful citizens." *The Telegraph*, 16 May 2010. http://www.telegraph.co.uk/news/science/7730522/Lying-children-will-grow-up-to-be-successful-citizens.html (accessed 24 August 2017).

Am I rich. No date. https://irememberthepoor.org/3-2/ (accessed 24 August 2017).

"American Lifestyles Mix Compassion and Self-Oriented Behavior." *Barna*, 5 February 2007. https://www.barna.com/research/american-lifestyles-mix-compassion-and-self-oriented-behavior/ (accessed 21 August 2017).

Ariely, Dan, Niel Garret, Stephanie C Lazzaro, and Tali Sharot. "The Brain Adapts to Dishonesty." *Nature Neuroscience.* Vol. 19 (2016) pp. 1727-1732.

Atheist Alliance International. Diaz, Carlos, and John Hamill. *AAI Gender Balance Report.* 2015.

Atkinson, Rowan. "Rowan Atkinson: we must be allowed to insult each other." *The Telegraph*, 18 October 2012. http://www.telegraph.co.uk/news/uknews/law-and-order/9616750/Rowan-Atkinson-we-must-be-allowed-to-insult-each-other.html (accessed 28 August 2017).

Augustine of Hippo. *Confessions*. Book 10, Chapter 23. No date.

Australian Associated Press. "Children of same-sex couples healthier, says Australian study." *The Guardian*, 7 July 2014. https://www.theguardian.com/world/2014/jul/07/ (accessed 21 August 2017).

Badenhorst, Nadene. "Hate Crimes & Hate Speech Bill Fraught with Problems!" *FOR SA*, 11 November 2016. https://forsa.org.za/hate-crimes-hate-speech-bill-fraught-with-problems/ (accessed 25 July 2017).

Barna Survey. "American Lifestyles Mix Compassion and Self-Oriented Behavior." 5 February 2007. https://www.barna.com/research/american-lifestyles-mix-compassion-and-self-oriented-behavior/ (accessed 21 August 2017).

Barna Survey. "New Marriage and Divorce Statistics Released." 21 March 2008. https://www.barna.com/research/new-marriage-and-divorce-s (accessed 24 August 2017).

Barna Survey. "The End of Absolutes: America's New Moral Code." 25 May 2016. https://www.barna.com/research/the-end-of-absolutes-americas-new-moral-code/ (accessed 24 August 2017).

Barnabas Fund. "UK Foreign Office agency says Evangelical Christians in the Global South should 'reinterpret' the Bible." https://barnabasfund.org/news/UK-Foreign-Office-agency-says-Evangelical-Christians-in-the-Global-South-should-reinterpret-the-Bible (accessed 21 August 2017).

Barrett, Lisa Feldman. "When is Speech Violence?" *New York Times*, 14 July 2017. https://www.nytimes.com/2017/07/14/opinion/sunday/when-is-speech-violence.html

Bath University. "Research shows how Christians can fall prey to consumerism." 22 August 2011. http://www.bath.ac.uk/news/2011/08/22/christianity-consumerism (accessed 31 July 2017).

BBC News. "US Christians numbers 'decline sharply', poll finds." 12 May 2015. http://www.bbc.co.uk/news/world-us-canada-32710444 (accessed 24 August 2017).

Beek, Kurt Ver. "The Impact of Short-Term Missions: A Case Study of House Construction in Honduras after Hurricane Mitch." *Missiology: An International Review*. Vol. 34, No. 4 (2006) pp. 477-495.

Bell, Rob, and Kirsten Bell. Interview by Oprah Winfrey. *Super Soul Sunday*, 15 February 2015). https://www.youtube.com/watch?v=_kyk3bf2Ac8 (accessed 24 August 2017).

Benen, Steve. "Dobson Points to Culture War Defeat." *Washington Monthly*, 12 April 2009.

Bercot, David. *Will the Real Heretics Please Stand Up: A New Look at Today's Evangelical Church in the Light of Early Christianity.* Tyler: Scroll Publishing, 1999.

Berlin, Isaiah. *Karl Marx.* Princeton: Princeton University Press, 2013.

Berlinger, Joshua. "Australians Ditch Religion at Rapid Rate, Becoming More Diverse." *CNN.* 28 June 2017. http://edition.cnn.com/2017/06/27/asia/australia-census-2016/index.html (accessed 25 July 2017).

Berrien, Hank. "Canada Passes Anti-Islamophobia Bill." *The Daily Wire.* 23 March 2017. http://www.dailywire.com/news/14740/canada-passes-anti-islamophobia-bill-hank-berrien#exit-modal (accessed 24 August 2017).

Bevans, Stephen B. *Models of Contextual Theology.* New York: Orbis, 1992.

Biblarz, Timothy, and Judith Stacey. "How Does the Gender of Parents Matter." *Journal of Marriage and the Family.* Vol. 72, No. 1 (2010) pp. 3-22.

Bilezikian, Gilbert. *Community 101: Reclaiming the Local Church as Community of Oneness.* Grand Rapids: Zondervan, 1997.

Borthwick, Paul. *Western Christians in Global Mission.* Downers Grove: InterVarsity Press, 2012.

Brueggemann, Walter. *The Covenanted Self: Explorations in Law and Covenant.* Minneapolis: Fortress Press, pp. 91-92.

Britannica. "Postmodernism." *Britannica.* 31 October 2014. https://global.britannica.com/topic/postmodernism-philosophy (accessed 24 August 2017).

Bullard, Gabe. "The World's Newest Major Religion: No Religion." *National Geographic*, 22 April 2016. http://news.nationalgeographic.com/2016/04/160422-atheism-agnostic-secular-nones-rising-religion/ (accessed 28 August 2017).

Bunker, S. J., D.M. Colquhoun, M.D. Esler, et al. "'Stress' and coronary heart disease: psychosocial risk factors. National Heart Foundation of Australia position statement update." *Medical Journal of Australia*. Vol. 178 (2003) pp. 272-276.

Business Insider. Speiser, Matthew. "Christians are Leaving The Faith in Droves and the Trend isn't Slowing Down." 28 April 2015. http://www.businessinsider.com/christians-are-leaving-the-faith-in-droves-2015-4 (accessed 28 August 2017).

Cadwalladr, Carole. "Google, democracy and the truth about internet search." *The Guardian*, December 4, 2016. https://www.theguardian.com/technology/2016/dec/04/google-democracy-truth-internet-search-facebook (accessed 9 August 2017).

Callincos, A. *Against Postmodernism: A Marxist Critique*. Cambridge: Polity Press, 1989.

Cambridge Dictionary. 'Snowflake generation.' http://dictionary.cambridge.org/dictionary/english/snowflake-generation (accessed 31 July 2017).

"Canadian District Bans Christian School from Teaching 'Offensive' Parts of Bible." *CBN News*, 22 June 2017. http://www1.cbn.com/cbnnews/world/2017/june/canadian-district-bans-christian-school-from-teaching-offensive-parts-of-bible-nbsp (accessed 28 August 2017).

Carson, D. A. The *Gagging of God: Christianity Confronts Pluralism*. Grand Rapids: Zondervan, 2011.

Carter, Sherrie Bourg. "Helper's High: The Benefits (and Risks) of Altruism." *Psychology Today*, 4 September 2014. https://www.psychologytoday.com/blog/high-octane-women/201409/helpers-high-the-benefits-and-risks-altruism (accessed 21 August 2017)

"Catholic school settles case that pit gay rights against religious liberty." *New Boston Post*, 10 May 2016. http://newbostonpost.com/2016/05/10/catholic-school-settles-case-that-pit-gay-rights-against-religious-liberty (accessed 24 August 2017).

Chan, Simon. "The Christian Identity: A Theological Perspective." *Church and Society in Asia Today.* Vol. 13, No. 3 (2010) pp. 123-131.

Chandler, Diana. "Affirm LGBT lifestyles, foster care workers ordered." *Baptist Press,* 1 June 2017. http://www.bpnews.net/48966/affirm-lgbt-lifestyles-foster-care-workers-ordered (accessed 24 August 2017).

Character Education Committee. American Association of School Administrators, 1932.

Charles, Tyler. "The Secret Sexual Revolution." *Relevant Magazine,* September/ October 2011.

Chong, Shiao. "Have it Your Way? When the Church Embraces Consumerism." The Banner, April 22, 2002, 28-30. Also published as "Consumerism and the Church" June 5, 2015 https://3dchristianity.wordpress.com/2015/06/05/consumerism-and-the-church/ (accessed 21 August 2017)

Christian Concern. "Christian Couple Blocked from Adopting Because of their Belief that Children Need Mum and Dad." 9 November 2016. http://www.christianconcern. com/our-concerns/adoption/foster-parents-prevented-from-adoption-because-they-believe-a-child-should-hav (accessed 29 August 2017).

Christian Today. "Pop stars tweet prayers after several killed in explosion at Ariana Grande concert in UK." 23 May 2017. https://www.christiantoday.com/article/pop.stars.tweet.prayers.several.killed.in.explosion.at.ariana.grande.concert.in.uk/109374.htm. (accessed 10 August 2017).

Christianity Today. "Tyndale Releases Results of Mark Driscoll Plagiarism Investigation." 18 December 2013. http://www.christianitytoday.com/news/2013/december/.html (accessed 28 August 2017).

Christianity Today. "5 Lies Pastors are Tempted to Tell – and How to Resist Them." 9 September 2016. http://www.christianitytoday.com/karl-vaters/2016/september/5-lies-pastors-are-tempted-to-tell-and-how-resist-them.html (accessed 28 August 2017).

Christianity Today. "The Leadership survey on Pastors and Internet Pornography." 2001. http://www.christianitytoday.com/pastors/2001/winter/12.89.html (accessed 28 August 2017).

Chumley, Cheryl, and Alex Swoyer. "Big surprise: Gay parents give kids better 'general health,' says scientific report by gay dad." *The Washington Times*, 7 July 2014. http://www.washingtontimes.com/news/2014/jul/7/gay-parents-give-kids-better-general-health-tradit/ (accessed 18 August 2017).

Church Urban Fund. "Bias to the Poor? Christian Attitudes to Poverty in this Country." January 2012. http://www2.cuf.org.uk/sites/default/files/PDFs/Research/Bias_to_the_poor_Jan2012.pdf (accessed 21 August 2017)

Churchill, Laura. "Street preachers arrested in front of cheering Bristol crowd were there to 'pick a fight'." *Bristol Post*, 23 February 2017. http://www.bristolpost.co.uk/news/bristol-news/street-preachers-arrested-front-cheering-2656 (accessed 10 August 2017).

Clinton, Bill. *The President's Radio Address* (23 March 1996).

CNN. Stetzer, Ed. "The rise of evangelical 'nones'." 15 June 2015. http://edition.cnn.com/2015/06/12/living/stetzer-christian-nones/index.html (accessed 28 August 2017).

"Code of Conduct on Countering Illegal Hate Speech Online." *European Commission*, 2016. http://www.west-info.eu/pdf/european-commission-code-of-conduct-on-countering-illegal-hate-speech-online-2016/ (accessed 24 August 2017)

Colbert, Stephen, interview by Nathan Rabin. *AV Club*, 25 January 2006.

Collins Dictionary. 'Snowflake generation.' https://www.collinsdictionary.com/dictionary/english/snowflake-generation (accessed 15 July 2017).

Comiskey, Joel. *2000 Years of Small Groups: A History of Cell Ministry in the Church*. Moreno Valley: CCS Publishing, 2015.

Cooper, Rob. "Forcing a religion on your children is as bad as child abuse, claims atheist professor Richard Dawkins." *Daily Mail*, 22 April 2013. http://www.dailymail.co.uk/news/article-2312813/Richard-Dawkins-Forcing-religion-children-child-abuse-claims-atheist-professor.html (accessed 10 August 2017).

Crouch, Simon. "Election Watch." 1 October 2014. http://past.electionwatch.edu.au/victoria-2014/it%E2%80%99s-time-adopt-change (accessed 27 January 2017).

Crouch, Simon. *Research Connect: Hidden agendas – do researchers and participants bring bias to studies?* 2014. https://researchconnect.wordpress.com/author/simonrcrouch/ (accessed 26 January 2017).

Crouch, Simon, Elizabeth Waters, Ruth McNair, Jennifer Power, and Elise Davis. "Parent-reported measures of child health and wellbeing in same-sex parent families: a cross-sectional survey." *BioMed Central Public Health*. June 2014. https://bmcpublichealth.biomedcentral.com/articles/10.1186/1471-2458-14-635 (accessed 24 August 2017).

Crown Prosecution Service. *Hate Crime What is it?* 2017. http://www.cps.gov.uk/northeast/victims_and_witnesses/hate_crime/ (accessed 10 August 2017).

Dawkins, Richard. *The God Delusion*. Boston: Houghton Mifflin Company, 2006.

Dawkins, Richard. "Forcing a religion on your children is as bad as child abuse, claims atheist professor Richard Dawkins." *Daily Mail*, 22 April 2013. http://www.dailymail.co.uk/news/article-2312813/Richard-Dawkins-Forcing-religion-children-child-abuse-claims-atheist-professor.html (accessed 10 August 2017).

Dawn, Marva J. *A Royal "Waste" of Time: The Spendor of Worshipping God and Being Church for the World*. Grand Rapids, Michigan: Eerdmans, 1999, pp. 1, 297.

Degeneres, Ellen. "Emmy Awards." 4 November 2001.

Dell, Josh. "UK Jewish school risks closure for refusal to teach LGBT issues." *Jerusalem Post*, 29 June 2017. http://www.jpost.com/Diaspora/British-Jewish-school-risks-closure-for-refusal-to-teach-LGBT-issues-498177 (accessed 10 July 2017).

Diaz, Carlos, and John Hamill. *AAI Gender Balance Report*. Washington DC: Atheist Alliance International, 2015.

Dreher, Rod. *The Benedict Option: A Strategy for Christians in a Post-Christian Nation*. New York: Sentinel, 2017, p. 77.

D'Souza, Joseph. "It's time for evangelicals to return to orthodoxy." *The Blaze*, 11 October 2016. http://www.theblaze.com/contributions/its-time-for-evangelicals-to-return-to-orthodoxy/ (accessed 19 August 2017).

Dunphy, John. "A Religion for a New Age." *The Humanist*, January-February 1983, p. 26.

Echersley, Richard. "Is Modern Western Culture a Health Hazard?" *International Journal of Epidemiology*. Vol. 35, No. 2 (2005) pp. 252-258.

Editors, The. "Facts and Figures: Healthier with Same-Sex Parents?" *The New York Times*, 7 July 2017. [I can't find the URL for this...have we got the right title?]

Empty Tomb. *The State of Church Giving through 2014: Speaking Truth to Power.* Champaign: Empty Tomb, 2016.

"European Hate Speech Laws." *The Legal Project*, 2017. http://www.legal-project.org/issues/european-hate-speech-laws (accessed 24 August 2017).

Experience a whole new culture and impact lives in the Bahamas! No date. http://www.shorttermmissions.com/trips/17480/ (accessed 1 August 2017).

Field, Clive. "Christian Attitudes to Poverty." *British Religion in Numbers*. 13 January 2012. http://www.brin.ac.uk/2012/christian-attitudes-to-poverty/ (accessed 10 August 2017)

Flemming, D. *Contextualisation in the New Testament: Paterns of Theology and Ministry.* Downers Grove: InterVarsity Press, 2005.

Forbes. "How big is Porn?" 25 May 2001. https://www.forbes.com/2001/05/25/0524porn.html (accessed 28 August 2017).

Forrester, D, Ian MacDonald, and Gian Tellini. *Encounter with Introduction to Christian Worship and Practice.* Edinburgh: T & T Clark, 1993.

Fox, Claire. "Generation Snowflake: how we train our kids to be censorious cry-babies." *The Spectator*, 4 June 2016. https://www.spectator.co.uk/2016/06/generation-snowflake-how-we-train-our-kids-to-be-censorious-cry-babies/ (accessed 31 July 2017).

Freedom of Religion South Africa. "Double Standards on Free Speech." https://forsa.org.za/double-standards-on-free-speech/ (accessed 28 August 2017).

Fuchs, Lorelei. *Koinonia and the Quest for an Ecumenical Ecclesiology.* Grand Rapids: Eerdmans, 2008.

Fukuyama, Francis. "Comment: The end of history? Well, certainly the end of humans." *The Independent*, 15 June 1999. http://www.independent.co.uk/arts-entertainment/comment-the-end-of-history-well-certainly-the-end-of-humans-1100380.html (accessed 24 August 2017).

Gallagher, Maggie. *National Review: Progressive Elites anti Christian Animus.* 20 February 2015. http://www.nationalreview.com/article/414149/progressive-elites-anti-christian-animus-maggie-gallagher (accessed 23 January 2017).

Gallup Study. "Gallup, statistics and discipleship." *TMATT.* 28 July 2004. http://www.tmatt.net/columns/2004/07/gallup-statistics-and-discipleship (accessed 10 August 2017).

Gessen, Masha. Radio interview. http://www.abc.net.au/radionational/programs/lifematters/why-get-married/4058506 (accessed 25 July 2017).

Gledhill, Ruth. "'God is good in the midst of evil.' Justin Bieber preaches it at Manchester concert." *Christian Today*, 4 June 2017. https://www.christiantoday.com/article/god.is.good.in.the.midst.of.evil.justin.bieber.preaches.it.at.manchester.concert/109784.htm. (accessed 24 August 2017).

Global Views on Morality. Pew Research Center on Religion and Public Life, 2013. http://www.pewglobal.org/2014/04/15/global-morality/ (accessed 24 August 2017).

God TV. "Justin Bieber Preaches at Manchester Benefit Concert: 'God is Good in the Midst of the Darkness'." 6 June 2017. https://godtv.com/justin-bieber-manchester-benefit-preach/ (accessed 24 August 2017).

Goheen, W. *"As the Father has sent me, I am sending you": J. E. Lesslie Newbigin's missionary ecclesiology.* Utrecht: Proefstrieft, 2001.

Goldingay, J. *Old Testament Theology Volume 3: Israel's Life.* Downers Grove: InterVarsity Press, 2009.

Gomes, Jules. "'Hate crime' is the product of our new secular religion." *The Conservative Woman*, 4 December 2016. http://www.conservativewoman.co.uk/rebel-priest-rev-jules-gomes-hate-crime-product-new-secular-religion/ (accessed 12 August 2017).

Gomes, Jules. "Apostate Church of England has mutated into a Gnostic 'Sex' Sect." *Virtue Online*, 20 July 2017. http://www.virtueonline.org/apostate-church-england-has-mutated-gnostic-sex-sect (accessed 23 July 2017).

Grant, Tobin. "The Great Decline: 61 years of religiosity in one graph, 2013 hits a new low." *Religion News Service*, 5 August 2014. http://religionnews.com/2014/08/05/the-great-decline-61-years-of-religion-religiosity-in-one-graph-2013-hits-a-new-low/ (accessed 21 August 2017)

Grip, Lars. "No Free Speech in Preaching: Swedish pastor sentenced to jail for blasting homosexuality." *Christianity Today*, 1 August 2004. http://www.christianitytoday.com/ct/2004/augustweb-only/8-9-12.0.html (accessed 24 August 2017).Groothuis, Douglas. *Truth Decay*. Illinois: Inter-Varsity Press, 2001.

Grossman, Cathy Lynn. "Has the 'notion of sin' been lost?" *USA Today*, 16 April 2008. http://usatoday30.usatoday.com/news/religion/2008-03-19-sin_N.htm (accessed 28 August 2017).

Gudmundsen, Richard. *Scientific Inquiry: Applied to the Doctrine of Jesus Christ.* Ceder Falls: Bonneville Books, 2009.

Gunter, Lorne. "The real threat behind M-103 is 'mission creep'." *The Toronto Sun*, 14 February 2017. http://www.torontosun.com/2017/02/14/the-real-threat-behind-m-103-is-mission-creep (accessed 24 August 2017).

Hadro, Matt. "Christian florist loses religious liberty case, will appeal to US Supreme Court." *Catholic News Service*, 16 February 2017. http://www.catholicnewsagency.com/news/christian-florist-loses-religious-liberty-case-will-appeal-to-us-supreme-court-57632/ (accessed 5 August 2017).

Haskell, David Millard, Kevin Flatt, and Stephanie Burgoyne. "Theology Matters: Comparing the Traits of Growing and Declining Mainline Protestant Church Attendees and Clergy." *Review of Religious Research.* Vol. 58, No. 4 (2016) pp.515-541.

Hasson, Mary. "Illinois purges Social Workers and Foster Families who don't 'Facilitate' Transgernderism" *The Federalist,* 30 May 2017. http://thefederalist.com/2017/05/30/illinois-purges-social-workers-foster-families-dont-facilitate-transgenderism/ (accessed 27 August 2017).

"Hate crime is becoming a weapon to use against Christians." *Barnabas Fund,* 12 January 2017. https://barnabasfund.org/news/Hate-crime-is-becoming-a-weapon-to-use-against-Christians (accessed 10 August 2017).

Haverluck, Michael. "US Barna Survey: Goodbye absolutes, hello new morality." *One News Now,* 29 May 2016. https://www.onenewsnow.com/culture/2016/05/29/us-barna-survey-goodbye-absolutes-hello-new-morality (accessed 24 August 2017).

Hellen, Nicholas. "Post Christian Britain arrives as majority say they have no religion." *The Times,* 17 January 2016. https://www.thetimes.co.uk/article/post-christian-britain-arrives-as-majority-say-they-have-no-religion-5bzxzdcl6p3 (accessed 24 August 2017).

Hestenes, J. *First Steps in Pactical Theology.* Pretoria: UNISA, 1999.

Hitchens, Christopher. *God is Not Great: How Religion Poisons Everything.* New York: Hachette Book Group, 2007.

Hitchens, Peter. *The Rage Against God.* London: Continuum, 2010, p.79.

Hofstede, Geert. *Culture's Consequences. Comparing Values, Behaviour, Institutions and Organisations across Nations.* London: Sage, 2001.

Holmes, Mike. "What Would Happen if the Church Tithed?" *Relevant,* 8 March 2016. https://relevantmagazine.com/god/church/what-would-happen-if-church-tithed (accessed 24 August 2017).

Howe, Jason. "EQCA: Equality California Announces Positions on November Ballot Initiatives." 26 September 2016. http://www.eqca.org/nov-init/ (accessed 27 January 2017).

Huffington Post. "Muslims 'Give Most To Charity', Ahead Of Christians, Jews And Atheists, Poll Finds." 3 October 2013. http://www.huffingtonpost.co.uk/2013/07/21/muslims-give-most_n_3630830.html (accessed 24 August 2017).

Huffington Post. "Pastors, Sermons and Plagiarism in the Internet Age." 6 August 2014. http://www.huffingtonpost.com/2014/06/08/sermon-plagiarism_n_5459855.html (accessed 24 August 2017).

Hunt, Stephen, Malcolm Hamilton, and Tony Walter (Editors). *Charismatic Christianity. Sociological Perspectives.* New York: St. Martin's Press, 1997.

Jacobs, James and Kimberly Potter. *Hate Crimes: Criminal Law and Identity Politics.* Oxford and New York: Oxford University Press, 1998, p. 6.

Janicaud, Dominique. *On the Human Condition: Thinking in Action.* London: Routledge, 2005.

Jenner, Richard. "Globalization, cultural symbols, and group consciousness: Culture as an adaptive complex system." *The Journal of New Paradigm Research.* Vol. 56, No. 1 (2000) pp. 21-39.

"Justin Bieber Preaches at Manchester Benefit Concert: 'God is Good in the Midst of the Darkness'." *God TV,* 6 June 2017. https://godtv.com/justin-bieber-manchester-benefit-preach/ (accessed 24 August 2017).

Keener, Craig. *Miracles: The Credibility of the New Testament Accounts.* Vol. 1. Grand Rapids: Baker Academic, 2011, pp. 83ff.

Keller, Timothy. Cited in "What Americans call Sin." *USA Today,* 19 march 2008. https://usatoday30.usatoday.com/news/religion/2008-03-19-sin_N.htm

Keller, Timothy. *Prayer: Experiencing Awe and Intimacy with God.* London: Hodder & Stoughton, 2014.

Kern, Soeren. "Belfast Pastor on Trial for Offending Islam." *Gladstone Institute*, 18 August 2015. https://www.gatestoneinstitute.org/6356/pastor-james-mcconnell-islam (accessed 18 August 2017).

Keyes, Ralph. *The Post Truth Era: Dishonesy in Contemporary Life.* 2004. http://www.ralphkeyes.com/the-post-truth-era/ (accessed 18 August 2017).

Keyserling, Hermann von. *American Set Free.* New York: Harper, 1929.

Kirk, Marshall, and Erastes Pill. "The Overhauling of Straight America." *Guide Magazine*, November 1987. http://library.gayhomeland.org/0018/EN/EN_Overhauling_Straight.htm (accessed 31 January 2017).

Kuby, Gabriele. *The Global Sexual Revolution: Destruction of Freedom in the Name of Freedom.* Translated by James Patrick Kirchner. Kettering, Ohio: Angelico Press, 2015, pp. 277-278.

Kunreuther, Frances, Barbara Masters, Gigi Barsoum, and Rebecca Fox. *At the Crossroads: The Future of the LGBT movement.* New York: Building Movement Project, 2013.

Lawrence, Joel. *Bonhoeffer: A Guide for the Perplexed.* London: T & T Clark, 2010.

Lee, Adam. "Godless Millennials Could End the Political Power of the Religious Right." *The Guardian*, 26 October 2014. https://www.theguardian.com/commentisfree/2014/oct/26/millennials-godless-politics-religous-conservatives (accessed 24 August 2017).

Leo, John. "The Politics of Hate." *U.S. News & World Report*, 9 October 1989, p. 24.

Limbaugh, Rush. "The Rush Limbaugh Show." 24 September 2012.

Lipka, Michael. "Americans' faith in God may be eroding." Pew Research Center on Religion and Public Life, 4 November 2015. http://www.pewresearch.org/fact-tank/2015/11/04/americans-faith-in-god-may-be-eroding/ (accessed 21 August 2017).

Lira, Kimberli. *A Young Widow's Story* "Why the church doesn't need anymore coffee bars.". 8 March 2017. http://kimberlilira.blogspot.co.za/2017/03/why-church-doesnt-need-anymore-coffee.html?m=1. (accessed 24 August 2017).

Lopez, Robert Oscar and Brittany Klein (editors). *Jephthah's Children: The Innocent Casualties of Same-Sex Parenting.* London: Wilberforce Publications, 2016, pp. 11, 24, 108-109, 241.

"Losing our religion? Two thirds of people still claim to be religious." *WINGIA*. 13 April 2015. http://www.wingia.com/en/news/losing_our_religion_two_thirds_of_people_still_claim_to_be_religious/290/ (accessed 28 August 2017).

Lukács, György. *History and Class Consciousness: Studies in Marxist Dialectics.* Translated by Rodney Livingstone, Cambridge, Mass.: The MIT Press, 1971, p. 111.

Lukács, György. *The Theory of The Novel: A historico-philosophical essay on the forms of great epic literature.* Translated by Anna Bostock. London: The Merlin Press, 1971.

Machen, J. Gresham. *Christianity and Liberalism.* Grand Rapids: Eerdmans, 1923.

Macy, Howard. "Community: God's Design For Growth." *Bible.org.* 29 May 2011. https://bible.org/article/community-god%E2%80%99s-design-growth (accessed 28 August 2017)

Marcuse, Herbert. *Eros and Civilization: A Philosophical Inquiry into Freud.* Boston, Massachusetts: Beacon Press, 1955.

Marx, Karl and Friedrich Engels. *The German Ideology.* London: Lawrence & Wishart Limited, 1970 (English translation).

Marx, Karl and Friedrich Engels. *The Communist Manifesto.* London: J. E. Burghard, 1848.

Mattil, Caitlyn. "5 Winning Strategies Feminists Can Learn From the Gay Rights Movement." 02 July 2013. https://mic.com/articles/52423/5-winning-strategies-feminists-can-learn-from-the-gay-rights-movement#.SqDsfHLPR (accessed 27 January 2017).

Mattingly, Terry. "Gallup, statistics and discipleship." *TMATT*. 28 July 2004. http://www.tmatt.net/columns/2004/07/gallup-statistics-and-discipleship (accessed 10 August 2017).

Mazur, Paul. *Harvard Business Review*, 1927.

McConnell, James cited in Soeren Kern, "Belfast Pastor on Trial for Offending Islam." *Gladstone Institute*, 18 August 2015. https://www.gatestoneinstitute.org/6356/pastor-james-mcconnell-islam (accessed 18 August 2017).

Mchanhama, Jacob. "The Problem with Hate Speech Laws." *The Review of Faith and International Affairs*. Vol. 13, No. 1 (2015) pp. 75-82.

Meacham, Jon. "The End of Christian America." *Newsweek*, 3 April 2009. http://www.newsweek.com/meacham-end-christian-america-77125 (accessed 28 August 2017).

Meister, Jeanne. "The Future Of Work: Job Hopping Is the 'New Normal' for Millennials." *Forbes*, 14 August 2012. https://www.forbes.com/sites/jeannemeister/2012/08/14/the-future-of-work-job-hopping-is-the-new-normal-for-millennials/#5ca94b8513b8 (accessed 21 August 2017).

Mohler, Albert. "Compromise and Confusion in the Churches." *Christian Headlines*. No Date. http://www.christianheadlines.com/columnists/al-mohler/compromise-and-confusion-in-the-churches-1317346.html (accessed 10 August 2017)

Mohler, Albert. "Criminalizing Christianity: Sweden's Hate Speech Law." *The Christian Post*. 6 August 2004. http://www.christianpost.com/news/criminalizing-christianity-sweden-s-hate-speech-law-6129/ (accessed 1 August 2017)

Moltmann, Jürgen. *The Crucified God: The Cross of Christ as the Foundation and Criticism of Christian Theology*. Munich: Christian Kaiser Verlag, 1973.

Moore, Russel. *Engaging the Culture without Losing the Gospel*. Nashville: B & H Publishing, 2015.

Morgenthaler, Sally. "Worship on the Edge." *Emerging Church*. 2012. www.emerging-church.org/Worship-on-the-edge.htm (accessed 5 August 2017)

Morley, Katie "Rise in legal battles over transgender children's rights." The Telegraph, 23 October 2016. http://www.telegraph.co.uk/news/2016/10/23/rise-in-legal-battles-over-transgender-childrens-rights/ (accessed 26 January 2018).

Moynihan, Carolyn. "Not so fast: That Australian study on gay parenting tells us almost nothing useful." 10 July 2014. https://www.lifesitenews.com/opinion/not-so-fast-that-australian-study-on-gay-parenting-tells-us-almost-nothing (accessed 27 January 2017).

Mullen, Peter. "Farewell, Church of England?" *The New Criterion*. Vol. 24, No. 1 (2005) pp.34-37.

Murphy, Caryle. "Most Americans believe in heaven … and hell." *Pew Reseach Center on Religion and Public Life*, 10 November 2015. http://www.pewresearch.org/fact-tank/2015/11/10/most-americans-believe-in-heaven-and-hell/ (accessed 10 August 2017).

Murray, Douglas. *The Strange Death of Europe: Immigration, Identity, Islam*. London: Bloomsbury, 2017, pp. 259, 264.

National Geographic. Bullard, Gabe. "The World's Newest Major Religion: No Religion." 22 April 2016. http://news.nationalgeographic.com/2016/04/160422-atheism-agnostic-secular-nones-rising-religion/ (accessed 28 August 2017).

NBC News. "Things are looking up in America's Porn Industry." 20 January 2015. https://www.nbcnews.com/business/business-news/things-are-looking-americas-porn-industry-n289431 (accessed 28 August 2017).

Niebuhr, H.Richard *The Kingdom of God in America*. New York: Harper & Row Publishers, 1937, p. 193.

Nietzsche, Friedrich. *Human, All-too-human*. Chemnitz: Ernst Schmeitzner, 1878.

Noack, Rich. "In this country, literally no young Christians believe that God created the Earth." *The Washington Post*, 23 January 2016. https://www.washingtonpost.com/news/worldviews/wp/2016/01/23/in-this-country-literally-no-young-christians-believe-that-god-created-the-earth/?utm_term=.5a43267b22f7 (accessed 28 August 2017).

Nolan, Clancy. *Patriotic Pride.* 2001. http://www.indyweek.com/indyweek/patriotic-pride/Content?oid=1184641 (accessed 23 January 2017).

Nouwen, Henri. *Here and Now: Living in the Spirit.* New York City: The Crossroad, 2006.

O'Brien, Zoie. "Church attendance drops to lowest rate EVER as UK faces 'anti-Christian' culture." *The Express*, 13 January 2016. http://www.express.co.uk/news/uk/634204/ (accessed 28 August 2017).

Olson, Roger. *The Mosaic of Christian Belief: Twenty Centuries of Unity and Diversity.* Downers Grove: InterVarsity Press, 2016.*Oxford Dictionary Word of the Year.* 2016. https://en.oxforddictionaries.com/word-of-the-year/word-of-the-year-2016 (accessed 12 July 2017).

Oxford Dictionary Word of the Year 2016. 2016. https://en.oxforddictionaries.com/word-of-the-year/word-of-the-year-2016 (accessed 12 July 2017).

Packer, J. I. "What is the future of Evangelicalism?: Evangelicalism Now." *Modern Reformation.* Vol. 17, No. 6 (2008).

Pariser, Eli. *The Filter Bubble: What the Internet is Hiding from You.* London: Penguin Books, 2011.

Park, A, C. Bryson and J. Curtice, "British Social Attitudes 31." *NatCen Social Research*, 2014. http://www.bsa.natcen.ac.uk/media/38893/bsa31_full_report.pdf (accessed 28 August 2017)

Paton, John. *John G. Paton, Missionary to the New Hebrides: An Autobiography.* New York: Carter, 1889.

Payne, Jon D. *In the Splendor of Holiness: Rediscovering the Beauty of Reformed Worship for the 21st Century* Dallas, Georgia: Tolle Lege Press, 2008.

Pearce, David. "The Hedonistic Imperative vs The Abolitionst Project. The Differences." *Institute for Ethics and Emerging Technologies*, 28 March 2014. https://ieet.org/index.php/IEET2/more/pearce20140328z (accessed 28 August 2017).

Peters, Mark. ""Alternative Facts"-and other helpful terms for political lies." *Boston Globe*. 26 January 2017. https://www.bostonglobe.com/ideas/2017/01/26/alternative-facts-and-other-helpful-terms-for-political-lies/yd3URC8mGSi7cAtUEs8BbN/story.html (accessed 28 August 2017).

Petre, Jonathan. "Christian foster parents condemn 'gay laws'." *The Telegraph*, 24 October 2007. http://www.telegraph.co.uk/news/uknews/1567160/Christian-foster-parents-condemn-gay-laws.html (accessed 28 August 2017).

Petrides, Alexis. "Manchester's heartbreak: 'I never grasped what big pop gigs were for until I saw one through my daughter's eyes.'" *The Guardian*, 23 May 2017. https://www.theguardian.com/uk-news/2017/may/23/manchester-heartbreak-never-grasped-what-big-pop-gigs-for-daughters-eyes

Pew Research Center on Religion and Public Life. "Religious Landscape Study." 2008. http://www.pewforum.org/religious-landscape-study/ (accessed 28 August 2017).

Pew Research Center on Religion and Public Life. "Nones on the Rise." 9 October 2012. http://www.pewforum.org/2012/10/09/nones-on-the-rise-demographics/ (accessed 28 August 2017).

Pew Research Center on Religion and Public Life. *Global Views on Morality*. 2013. http://www.pewglobal.org/2014/04/15/global-morality/ (accessed 24 August 2017).

Pew Research Center on Religion and Public Life. Lipka, Michael. "Americans' faith in God may be eroding." 4 November 2015. http://www.pewresearch.org/fact-tank/2015/11/04/americans-faith-in-god-may-be-eroding/ (accessed 21 August 2017).

Pope John Paul II. *The Holy See*. The Vatican, 2004.

Powers, Nicholas. *Truth Out: The "War on Terror" and Gay Marriage: How a Generation Turned Against Religious Extremism*. 2015. http://www.truth-out.org/news/item/33509-the-war-on-terror-and-gay-marriage-how-a-generation-turned-against-religious-extremism (accessed 23 January 23 2017).

Platt, David. *Radical: Taking Back Your Faith From the American Dream*. Colorado Springs: Multnomah Books, 2010.

Prest, Wilfred. *William Blackstone: Law and Letters in the Eighteenth Century.* New York: Oxford University Press, 2008.

Priest, Robert, Robert Dischinger, Steve Rasmussen, and C. M. Brown. "Researching the Short-Term Mission Movement." *Missiology: An International Review.* Vol. 34, No. 4 (2006) 431-450.

Proudhon, Pierre-Joseph. *The System of Economic Contradictions, or The Philosophy of Poverty.* Paris: Guillaum et Cie, 1846.

Psychology Today. Carter, Sherrie Bourg. "Helper's High: The Benefits (and Risks) of Altruism." 4 September 2014. https://www.psychologytoday.com/blog/high-octane-women/201409/helpers-high-the-benefits-and-risks-altruism (accessed 21 August 2017).

Puar, Jasbir K. *Terrorist Assemblages: Homonationalism in Queer Times.* Durham and London: Drake University Press, 2007.

Putnam, Hilary. *Realism and Reason: Philosophical Papers Volume 3.* Cambridge: Cambridge, 1983.

Rand, Ayn. *The Virtue of Selfishness: A collection of Essays.* Irvine: Ayn Rand Institute, 2017.

Regnerus, Mark. *Forbidden Fruit: Sex & Religion in the Lives of American Teenagers .* Oxford: Oxford University Press, 2007.

Reich, Wilhelm. *The Sexual Revolution: Toward a Self-Governing Character Structure.* New York: Farrar, Straus and Giroux, 1974.

"Religious Landscape Study." Pew Research Center on Religion and Public Life, 2008. http://www.pewforum.org/religious-landscape-study/ (accessed 28 August 2017).

"Research shows how Christians can fall prey to consumerism." *Bath University*, 22 August 2011. http://www.bath.ac.uk/news/2011/08/22/christianity-consumerism/ (accessed 31 July 2017).

Riddell, Mike, and Mark Pierson. *The Prodigal Project - Journey into the Emerging Church.* London: The Society For Promoting Christian Knowledge, 2000.

Rigoni, Brandon, and Bailey Nelson. "Few Millennials Are Engaged at Work." *Business Journal*, 2016. http://www.gallup.com/businessjournal/195209/few-millennials-engaged-work.aspx (accessed 28 August 2017).

Relevant Magazine. Charles, Tyler. "The Secret Sexual Revolution." September/October 2011.

Robbins, Gill. "A very unequal equality." *Christians in Education*, 23 June 2017. http://christiansineducation.co.uk/a-very-unequal-equality/ (accessed 28 August 2017).

Rose, Lacey. "Lying Is Good For You." *Forbes.* 24 October 2005. http://www.forbes.com/2005/10/19/lying-dishonesty-psychology_cx_lr_comm05_1024lie.html (accessed 10 July 2017).

Ross, Tim, Cole Moreton, and James Kirkup. "Former archbishop of Canterbury: We are a post-Christian nation." *The Telegraph*, 26 April 2014. http://www.telegraph.co.uk/news/religion/10790495/Former-archbishop-of-Canterbury-We-are-a-post-Christian-nation.html (accessed 28 August 2017).

Rubin, Edward L. *Soul, Self and Society: The New Morality and the Modern State.* Oxford: Oxford University Press, 2015.

Rudgard, Olivia. 'Britain has more non-believers than ever before as Church of England Christians make up lowest-ever share.' *The Telegraph,* 4 September 2017. http://www.telegraph.co.uk/news/2017/09/04/britain-has-non-believers-ever-church-england-christians-make/ (accessed 6 September 2017).

Sacks, Lord Jonathan, interview by BBC Radio 4. *The decline of religion in the West*, 26 June 2015.

Saine, Cindy. *Voice of America: Obama: Targeting of Gay Show Terrorist' intolerance.* 2016. http://www.voanews.com/a/obama-terrorist-groups-target-gays-and-lesbians/3374964.html (accessed 23 January 2017).

Sande, Ken. "The High Cost of Conflict Among Christians." *Peacemaker Ministries.* 18 February 2015. http://peacemaker.net/project/the-high-cost-of-conflict-among-christians/ (accessed 21 August 2017).

Schaeffer, Francis. *The Great Evangelical Disaster.* Wheaton: Crossway, 1984.

Schirripa, Jessica. "How This Generation's Obsession With Selfies Correlates With Mental Disorders." *Generation Y.* 19 Janurary 2015. http://elitedaily.com/life/selfies-self-love-surgeries/902152/ (accessed 29 July 2017).

Scotland, Nigel. "Shopping for a Church: Consumerism and the Churches." In *Christ and Consumerism: Critical Analysis of the Spirit of the Age*, edited by Craig Bartholomew, & Thorsten Moritz. Carlisle: Paternoster, 2000, pp.135-151.

Schweitzer, Maurice, and Emma Levine. "Is Every Lie 'a sin'? Maybe Not." *University of Pennsylvania*, 17 September 2014. http://knowledge.wharton.upenn.edu/article/when-lying-is-ethical/ (accessed 19 August 2017).

Sellars, Andrew. "Defining Hate Speech." *Berkman Klein Center Research Publication.* No. 2016-20, Boston University School of Law, Public Law Research Paper No. 16-48 2016.

Sherwood, Harriet. "Church of England weekly attendance falls below 1m for first time." *The Guardian*, 12 January 2016. https://www.theguardian.com/world/2016/jan/12/church-of-england-attendance-falls-below-million-first-time (accessed 21 August 2017).

Sherwood, Harriet. "Literal interpretation of Bible 'helps increase church attendance." *The Guardian*, 17 November 2016. https://www.theguardian.com/world/2016/nov/17/literal-interpretation-of-bible-helps-increase-church-attendance (accessed 28 August 2017).

Sherwood, Harriet. "UK Mennonites end Sunday services after numbers dwindle." *The Guardian*, 16 March 2016. https://www.theguardian.com/world/2016/mar/16/uk-mennonites-end-sunday-services-after-numbers-dwindle (accessed 28 August 2017).

Siedentop, Larry. *Inventing the Individual: The Origins of Western Liberalism.* Cambridge, Massachusetts: The Belknap Press of Harvard University Press, 2014.

Silverstein, Louise B. and Carl F. Auerbach. "Deconstructing the Essential Father." *American Psychologist*. Vol 45, No. 6 (1999) pp.397-407.

Smith, Christian with Melinda Lundquist Denton. *Soul Searching: The Religious and Spiritual Lives of American Teenagers*. New York: Oxford University Press, 2005, p. 266.

Smith, Christian and Michael Emerson. *Passing the Plate: Why American Christians Don't Give Away More Money*. New York: Oxford University Press, 2008, pp. 3, 175-177.

Smith. Christian, 'On "Moralistic Therapeutic Deism" as U.S. Teenagers' Actual, Tacit, De Facto Religious Faith' in *Religion and Youth*, edited by Sylvia Collins-Mayo and Pink Dandelion. Farnham, Surrey: Ashgate Publishing Ltd., 2010, pp. 46-48.

Sookhdeo, Patrick. *The New Civic Religion: Humanism and the Future of Christianity*. McLean, Virginia: Isaac Publishing, 2016.

Speiser, Matthew. "Christians are Leaving The Faith in Droves and the Trend isn't Slowing Down." *Business Insider*, 28 April 2015. http://www.businessinsider.com/christians-are-leaving-the-faith-in-droves-2015-4 (accessed 28 August 2017).

Spillis, Alex. "US religious Right concedes defeat." *The Telegraph*, 10 April 2009. http://www.telegraph.co.uk/news/worldnews/barackobama/5136050/US-religious-Right-concedes-defeat.html (accessed 28 August 2017).

Spurgeon, Charles. *The Complete Works of C. H. Spurgeon, Volume 32: Sermons 1877-1937.* Harrington: Delmarva Publications, 2013.

Stanford Encyclopedia of Philosophy. "Truth." https://plato.stanford.edu/entries/truth/ (accessed 28 August 2017).

Stark, Rodney. *The Rise of Christianity: How the Obscure, Marginal Jesus Movement Became the Dominant Religious Force in the Western World in a Few Centuries.* San Francisco: Harper Collins, 1997.

Staufenberg, Jess. "Majority of Norwegians 'do not believe in God' for first time in country's history." *The Independent*, 21 March 2016. http://www.independent.co.uk/

news/world/europe/norwegians-believe-in-god-majority-do-not-for-first-time-ever-a6943706.html (accessed 28 August 2017).

Steger, Manfred, *Globalization: A Very Short Introduction.* Oxford: Oxford University Press, 2003, p.10.

Stetzer, Ed. "The rise of evangelical 'nones'." *CNN,* 15 June 2015. http://edition.cnn.com/2015/06/12/living/stetzer-christian-nones/index.html (accessed 28 August 2017).

Stourton, Ed. "The Decline of Religion in the West." *BBC News,* 26 June 2015. http://www.bbc.com/news/world-33256561 (accessed 28 August 2017).

Strayhorn, Joseph M, and Jillian C Strayhorn. "Religiosity and teen birth rate in the United States." *Reproductive Health.* Vol 6. No. 14, 2009. https://reproductive-health-journal.biomedcentral.com/articles/10.1186/1742-4755-6-14 (accessed 28 August 2017).

Stuttaford, Andrew. ""Fake News", "Post-Truth" and All the Rest." *National Review,* 25 November 2016. http://www.nationalreview.com/corner/442472/fake-news-post-truth-and-all-rest (accessed 28 August 2017).

Swain, Michael. "Double Standards on Free Speech." *FORSA,* 21 June. https://forsa.org.za/double-standards-on-free-speech/ (accessed 28 August 2017).

"Swedish midwife loses fight to be exempt from performing abortions." *Fox News World,* 12 April 2017. http://www.foxnews.com/world/2017/04/12/swedish-midwife-loses-fight-to-be-exempt-from-performing-abortions.html (accessed 28 August 2017).

Sweet, Leonard. *The Greatest Story Never Told: Revive Us Again.* Nashville: Abington Press, 2012.

Taylor, Jenny. "After Ariana Grande & The Manchester Attacks: Three 'Unrealities' Are Killing Britain's Children." *The Media Project,* 30 May 2017. https://themediaproject.org/news/2017/5/30/after-ariana-grande-the-manchester-attacks-three-unrealities-are-killing-britains-children (accessed 21 August 2017).

Taylor, Jerome and Sarah Morrison. "The Islamification of Britain: record numbers embrace Muslim faith. " *The Independent*, 4 January 2011. http://www.independent. co.uk/news/uk/home-news/the-islamification-of-britain-record-numbers-embrace-muslim-faith-2175178.html (accessed 21 August 2017).

Tennent, Timothy. "The Challenge of Churchless Christianity: An Evangelical Assessment." *International Bulletin of Mission Research*. Vol. 29, No. 4, (2005) pp. 171-177.

The Christian Post. "Dramatic Fall of Christianity in UK Continues: 26 Christians Abandon Faith for Every One New Convert." Stoyan Zaimov, 15 May 2017. http://www. christianpost.com/news/dramatic-fall-of-christianity-in-uk-continues-26-christians-abandon-faith-for-every-one-new-convert-183598/ (accessed 25 July 2017).

The Constructivist Classroom and Curriculum. *Constructivist and Existentialist Education*, 14 March 2012. https://constructivismandexistentialism.wordpress.com/ (accessed 21 August 2017).

The Express. O'Brien, Zoie. "Church attendance drops to lowest rate EVER as UK faces 'anti-Christian' culture." 13 January 2016. http://www.express.co.uk/news/ uk/634204/ (accessed 28 August 2017)

"The 'Gay' Commentary on Same-Sex Marriage." http://www.albatrus.org/english/ lien_of_oz/homosexuality/gay_commentary_samesex_marriage.htm (accessed 14 August 2017).

The Guardian. Petrides, Alexis. "Manchester's heartbreak: 'I never grasped what big pop gigs were for until I saw one through my daughter's eyes.'" 23 May 2017. https:// www.theguardian.com/uk-news/2017/may/23/manchester-heartbreak-never-grasped-what-big-pop-gigs-for-daughters-eyes

The Guardian. "Children of same-sex couples healthier, says Australian study." 7 July 2014. https://www.theguardian.com/world/2014/jul/07/ (accessed 21 August 2017).

The Guardian. "Church of England weekly attendance falls below 1m for first time." 12 January 2016. https://www.theguardian.com/world/2016/jan/12/church-of-england-attendance-falls-below-million-first-time (accessed 21 August 2017).

The Guardian. Sherwood, Harriet. "UK Mennonites end Sunday services after numbers dwindle." 16 March 2016. https://www.theguardian.com/world/2016/mar/16/uk-mennonites-end-sunday-services-after-numbers-dwindle (accessed 28 August 2017).

The Guardian. Sherwood, Harriet. "Literal interpretation of Bible 'helps increase church attendance." 17 November 2016. https://www.theguardian.com/world/2016/nov/17/literal-interpretation-of-bible-helps-increase-church-attendance (accessed 28 August 2017).

The Guardian. Cadwalladr, Carole. "Google, democracy and the truth about internet search." December 4, 2016. https://www.theguardian.com/technology/2016/dec/04/google-democracy-truth-internet-search-facebook (accessed 9 August 2017).

The Guardian. "Sean Spicer Defends Inauguration Claim." 23 January 2017. https://www.theguardian.com/us-news/2017/jan/23/sean-spicer-white-house-press-briefing-inauguration-alternative-facts (accessed 9 August 2017).

The Independent. "The Islamification of Britain: record numbers embrace Muslim faith." 4 January 2011. http://www.independent.co.uk/news/uk/home-news/the-islamification-of-britain-record-numbers-embrace-muslim-faith-2175178.html (accessed 21 August 2017).

"The Leadership survey on Pastors and Internet Pornography." *Christianity Today*, 2001. Originally published in *Leadership Journal*. Winter 2001. http://www.christianitytoday.com/pastors/2001/winter/12.89.html (accessed 28 August 2017).

The Legal Project. "European Hate Speech Laws." http://www.legal-project.org/issues/european-hate-speech-laws (accessed 28 August 2017).

The Spectator. Thompson, Damian. "2067: The End of British Christianity." 13 June 2015. https://www.spectator.co.uk/2015/06/2067-the-end-of-british-christianity/ (accessed 28 August 2017).

The Telegraph. Alleyne, Richard. "Lying children will grow up to be successful citizens." 16 May 2010. http://www.telegraph.co.uk/news/science/7730522/Lying-children-will-grow-up-to-be-successful-citizens.html (accessed 24 August 2017).

The Telegraph. "Rowan Atkinson: we must be allowed to insult each other." 18 October 2012. http://www.telegraph.co.uk/news/uknews/law-and-order/9616750/Rowan-Atkinson-we-must-be-allowed-to-insult-each-other.html (accessed 28 August 2017).

The Telegraph. "Victorian family values are a myth, Archbishop tells Mothers' Union." 23 September 2016. http://www.telegraph.co.uk/news/2016/09/23/victorian-family-values-are-a-myth-archbishop-tells-mothers-unio/ (accessed 29 August 2017).

The Telegraph. Morley, Katie. "Rise in legal battles over transgender children's rights." 23 October 2016. http://www.telegraph.co.uk/news/2016/10/23/rise-in-legal-battles-over-transgender-childrens-rights/ (accessed 26 January 2018).

The Times. Hellen, Nicholas. "Post Christian Britain arrives as majority say they have no religion." 17 January 2016. https://www.thetimes.co.uk/article/post-christian-britain-arrives-as-majority-say-they-have-no-religion-5bzxzdcl6p3 (accessed 24 August 2017).

The Washington Post. Noack, Rich. "In this country, literally no young Christians believe that God created the Earth." 23 January 2016. https://www.washingtonpost.com/news/worldviews/wp/2016/01/23/in-this-country-literally-no-young-christians-believe-that-god-created-the-earth/?utm_term=.5a43267b22f7 (accessed 28 August 2017).

The Washington Times. Chumley, Cheryl, and Alex Swoyer. "Big surprise: Gay parents give kids better 'general health,' says scientific report by gay dad." 7 July 2014. http://www.washingtontimes.com/news/2014/jul/7/gay-parents-give-kids-better-general-health-tradit/ (accessed 18 August 2017).

Thompson, Damian. "2067: The End of British Christianity." *The Spectator,* 13 June 2015. https://www.spectator.co.uk/2015/06/2067-the-end-of-british-christianity/ (accessed 28 August 2017).

Time. "Is God Dead." 8 April 1966.

Tooley, Hannah. "Archbishop of Canterbury: traditional Victorial family values 'a myth.'" *Premier Radio,* September 23, 2016. https://www.premier.org.uk/News/UK/Archbishop-of-Canterbury-traditional-Victorian-family-values-a-myth (accessed 10 August 2017).

Tozer, A. W. *The Attributes of God*. Camp Hill: Wingspread, 2003.

Travis, J, R. Brown, et al. "Movements and Contextualisation: Is there really a Correlation?" *International journal of Frontier Missiology*. Vol. 26, No. 1 (2009) pp. 21-23.

Tuschik, Kerstin. "Injustice via the Internet: Myths, Facts, & Smear Campaigns in the Marc Gafni Story: An Exposé by Kerstin Tuschik" https://ciw.s3.amazonaws.com/Kerstin-Tuschik-Expose-Marc-Gafni-Story.pdf (accessed on 28 August 2017).

Twenge, Jean M., Elise C. Freeman, and W. Keith Campbell. "Generational Differences in Young Adults' Life Goals, Concern for Others, and Civic Orientation, 1966-2009."; *Journal of Personality and Social Psychology*, Vol. 102, No. 5. (2012) pp.1045-1062.

Unwin, Joseph. *Sex and Culture*. London: Oxford University Press, 1934.

Urban, Rebecca. "Christians under siege, religious freedom inquiry hears." *The Australian*, 6 May 2017.

Vaidhyanathan, Siva. *The Googlization of Everything (and Why We Should Worry)*. Berkeley, Los Angeles: University of California Press, 2011, pp. xi, 6.

Vaters, Karl. "5 Lies Pastors are Tempted to Tell – and How to Resist Them." *Christianity Today*, 9 September 2016. http://www.christianitytoday.com/karl-vaters/2016/september/5-lies-pastors-are-tempted-to-tell-and-how-resist-them.html (accessed 28 August 2017).

Veith, Gene Edward. "Sex and the evangelical teen." *World Magazine*, 11 August 2007. https://world.wng.org/2007/08/sex_and_the_evangelical_teen (accessed 28 August 2017).

Walker, Andrew. "Thoroughly Modern Sociological Reflections on the Charismatic Movement from the End of the Twentieth Century," in Hunt, Hamilton and Walker (eds.) *Charismatic Christianity*. London: Palgrave Macmillan, 1997, pp. 17-41. 30.

Walker, Peter. "Christians' discrimination cases rejected by human rights court." *The Guardian*, 28 May 2013. https://www.theguardian.com/world/2013/may/28/christians-discrimination-cases-rejected-human-rights-court (accessed 21 August 2017).

Weatherbe, Steve. "Christian bakers raise $355,000: were forced to close store after refusing to bake same-sex 'wedding' cake." *Life Site*. 15 July 2015. https://www.lifesitenews.com/news/christian-bakers-raise-355000-will-appeal-oregon-discrimination-fine (accessed 21 August 2017).

Webber, Robert E. "An Evangelical and Catholic Methodology." *Religion Online*, No date. http://www.religion-online.org/showarticle.asp?title=14 (accessed 10 July 2017).

Webber, Robert E. *Ancient Future Worship*. Grand Rapids: Baker Publishing Group, 2008.

Welby, Justin. "Archbishop of Canterbury's address to the Primates gathering." *Anglican Ink*, 11 January 2016. http://www.anglican.ink/article/archbishop-canterburys-address-primates-gathering (accessed 24 August 2017).

Wells, David. *God in the Wasteland: The Reality of Truth in a World of Fading Dreams*. Grand Rapids: Eerdmans, 1994.

Wesley, John. *The Works of the Reverend John Wesley*. New York: B. Waugh and T. Mason, 1835.

Whewell, Tim. "Norway's Barnevernet: They took our four children... then the baby." *BBC News*, 14 April 2016. http://www.bbc.com/news/magazine-36026458 (accessed 8 August 2017).

White, Susan. "A New Story to Live By?" *Transmission*, 1998.

Willimon, William H. *Worship as Pastoral Care*. Nashville: Abingdon Press, 1993.

Wilson, Nate. "The Essentials of the Kerygma: What We Must Preach." *Nate Wilson Family*. January 2001. http://www.natewilsonfamily.net/kerygma.html (accessed 5 August 2017).

Wilton Park. "Opportunities and Challenges: The intersection of faith and human rights of LGBTI+ persons." https://www.wiltonpark.org.uk/wp-content/uploads/WP1488-Report.pdf (accessed 28 August 2017).

Wood, Keith Porteous cited in Peter Walker, "Christians' discrimination cases rejected by human rights court." *The Guardian*, 28 May 2013. https://www.theguardian.com/world/2013/may/28/christians-discrimination-cases-rejected-human-rights-court (accessed 28 August 2017).

World Magazine. Veith, Gene Edward. "Sex and the evangelical teen." 11 August 2007. https://world.wng.org/2007/08/sex_and_the_evangelical_teen (accessed 28 August 2017).

Wright, George, ed. *The Works of George Berkeley Bishop of Cloyne*. Glasgow: R Griffin and Co, 1843.

Wright, N. T. *Simply Christian: Why Christianity Makes Sense*. San Francisco: HarperOne, 2006.

Wright, N. T. *Pauline Perspectives: Essays on Paul 1978-213*. London: Society for Promoting Christian Knowledge, 2013.

Yancey, George, and David Williamson. *So Many Christians, So Few Lions: Is There Christianophobia in the United States?* London: Rowman & Littlefield, 2015.

Zaimov, Stoyan. "Christian-Run Nursing Home in Switzerland Forced to Allow Assisted Suicide or Lose Charitable Status." *The Christian Post*, 28 October 2016. http://www.christianpost.com/news/christian-run-nursing-home-switzerland-forced-allow-assisted-suicide-lose-charitable-status-171161/ (accessed 21 August 2017).

Zaimov, Stoyan. "Dramatic Fall of Christianity in UK Continues: 26 Christians Abandon Faith for Every One New Convert." *Christian Post*, 15 May 2017. http://www.christianpost.com/news/dramatic-fall-of-christianity-in-uk-continues-26-christians-abandon-faith-for-every-one-new-convert-183598 (accessed 25 July 2017).

Zimmermann, Jens. "Western Culture after Christendom." *The Humanist Lens*, 5 February 2011. http://www.humanismandculture.com/chapter-1-western-culture-after-christendom/ (accessed 29 August 2017).

INDEX OF BIBLICAL REFERENCES

INDEX